EXPLORING
ENGLISH

4

EXPLORING ENGLISH

4

Tim Harris • Allan Rowe

Longman

Exploring English 4

A Pearson Education Company
Pearson Education
10 Bank Street
White Plains, NY 10606

Editorial director: Joanne Dresner
Acquisitions editor: Anne Boynton-Trigg
Production editor: Nik Winter
Text design: Curt Belshe
Cover design: Curt Belshe
Cover illustration: Allan Rowe

ISBN 0-201-82578-3

Library of Congress Cataloging-in-Publication Data

Harris, Tim.
    Exploring English / Tim Harris; illustrated by Allan Rowe.
      p.   cm.
    1. English language—Textbooks for foreign speakers.   I. Rowe,
Allan.   II. Title.
PE1128.H347   1995
428.2'4—dc20   94-47408
                                                         CIP

15 – BAM – 04 03

To our families

Contents

Preface

Exploring English is a comprehensive, six-level course for adult and young adult students of English. It teaches all four language skills—listening, speaking, reading, and writing—with an emphasis on oral communication. The course combines a strong grammar base with in-depth coverage of language functions and life skills.

Exploring English:

Teaches grammar inductively. The basic structures are introduced in context through illustrated situations and dialogues. Students use the structures in talking about the situations and re-enacting the dialogues. They encounter each structure in a variety of contexts, including practice exercises, pair work activities, and readings. This repeated exposure enables students to make reliable and useful generalizations about the language. They develop a "language sense"—a feeling for words—that carries over into their daily use of English.

Includes language functions in every chapter from beginning through advanced levels. Guided conversations, discussions, and role plays provide varied opportunities to practice asking for and giving information, expressing likes and dislikes, agreeing and disagreeing, and so on.

Develops life skills in the areas most important to students: food, clothing, transportation, work, housing, and health care. Everyday life situations provide contexts for learning basic competencies: asking directions, taking a bus, buying food, shopping for clothes, and so on. Students progress from simpler tasks, such as describing occupations at the beginning level, to interviewing for jobs and discussing problems at work at more advanced levels.

Incorporates problem solving and critical thinking in many of the lessons, especially at the intermediate and advanced levels. The stories in *Exploring English* present a cast of colorful characters who get involved in all kinds of life problems, ranging from personal relationships to work-related issues to politics. Students develop critical-thinking skills as they discuss these problems, give their opinions, and try to find solutions. These discussions also provide many opportunities for students to talk about their own lives.

Provides extensive practice in listening comprehension through illustrated situations. Students are asked to describe each illustration in their own words before listening to the accompanying story (which appears on the reverse side of the page). Then they answer questions based on the story, while looking at the illustration. The students respond to what they see and hear without referring to text, just as they would in actual conversation.

Offers students frequent opportunities for personal expression. The emphasis throughout *Exploring English* is on communication—encouraging students to use the language to express their own ideas and feelings. Free response questions in Books 1 and 2 give students the opportunity to talk about themselves using simple, straightforward English. Every chapter in Books 3–6 has a special section, called "One Step Further," that includes discussion topics such as work, leisure activities, cinema, travel, dating, and marriage. Ideas for role plays are also provided to give additional opportunities for free expression. The general themes are familiar to students because they draw on material already covered in the same chapter. Role plays give students a chance to interact spontaneously—perhaps the most important level of practice in developing communication skills.

Provides continuous review and reinforcement. Each chapter concludes with a review section and every fourth chapter is devoted entirely to review, allowing students to practice newly acquired language in different combinations.

Provides exposure to key structures that students will be learning at the next level. This material, included in a special unit called "Preview," can be introduced at any time during the course at the discretion of the teacher.

Presents attractive art that visually supports and is integral with the language being taught. Humorous and imaginative illustrations, in full color, make *Exploring English* fun for students. In addition, the richness of the art allows teachers to devise their own spin-off activities, increasing the teachability of each page.

Each volume of *Exploring English* is accompanied by a Workbook. The Workbook lessons are closely coordinated with the lessons in the Student Book. They provide additional writing practice using the same grammatical structures and vocabulary while expanding on basic functions and life skills. The activities range from sentence completion exercises to guided paragraph and composition writing.

Student Books and Workbooks include clear labels and directions for each activity. In addition, Teacher's Resource Manuals are available for each level. These Manuals provide step-by-step guidance for teaching each page, expansion activities, and answers to the exercises. Each student page is reproduced for easy reference.

Audiocassettes for each level featuring an entertaining variety of native voices round out the series. All of the dialogues, readings, and pronunciation exercises are included on the tapes.

Chapter 1

TOPICS
People and cities
Jobs and employers

GRAMMAR
Comparative

FUNCTIONS
Making comparisons
Agreeing and disagreeing
Talking about feelings
Complaining
Sympathizing

1

2

1. Talk about the pictures.
2. Listen to the stories.
3. Answer the story questions.

READING

1 Albert is twenty years old and Jimmy is seventeen. Albert is older than Jimmy. He's also heavier. He weighs 175 pounds. Jimmy only weighs 150 pounds. Jimmy is younger and thinner than Albert. And he's taller. Jimmy is five feet ten inches tall. Albert is only five feet seven inches tall.

1. Who's older, Albert or Jimmy?
2. Which one is heavier?
3. How much does Albert weigh?
4. How much does Jimmy weigh?
5. Is Albert taller than Jimmy?
6. How tall is Albert?
7. How tall is Jimmy?

2 San Francisco and Los Angeles are both large cities. But Los Angeles is larger than San Francisco. It has a population of almost three million people. The population of San Francisco is less than one million. Los Angeles has very good weather. The weather in Los Angeles is better than in San Francisco. But the air in Los Angeles is bad. It's worse than in San Francisco.

1. Which of the two cities is larger?
2. What's the population of Los Angeles?
3. What's the population of San Francisco?
4. Which city has better weather?
5. Is the air better in Los Angeles than in San Francisco?

SHORT-WORD COMPARATIVE

Albert is older than Jimmy.

_____ bigger _____ .

_____ heavier _____ .

_____ shorter _____ .

WRITTEN EXERCISE • *Complete the sentences, using the comparative form.*

Jimmy is (tall) _*taller*_ than Albert.

The air in Los Angeles is (bad) _*worse*_ than in San Francisco.

1. Tino is (strong) _____ than Johnnie.

2. Mabel is (heavy) _____ than Linda.

3. A bicycle is (cheap) _____ than a motorcycle.

4. An airplane is (fast) _____ than a car.

5. Mr. Bascomb is (rich) _____ than Dr. Pasto.

6. Sam is (busy) _____ than Jack.

7. These glasses are (clean) _____ than those.

8. Your lessons are (easy) _____ than mine.

9. The weather in Los Angeles is (good) _____ than in San Francisco.

Listen and practice.

MABEL: Do you think Sunnyville is better than Fast City?

SAM: Sure. People are nicer in Sunnyville.

MABEL: But isn't it expensive there?

SAM: Sunnyville is cheaper than Fast City.

MABEL: What about the weather?

SAM: It's better in Sunnyville.

MABEL: Then why do some people prefer Fast City?

SAM: I don't know. I can't understand it.

FREE RESPONSE • *Would you prefer to live in Sunnyville or Fast City? Why?*

SUNNYVILLE   population: 42,106   FAST CITY   population: 537,853

PAIR WORK • *Ask and answer questions about the two cities using the comparative form.*

> friendly
> A. **Which city is friendlier?**
> B. **Sunnyville (is).**

1. clean   4. noisy   7. large
2. busy   5. safe   8. cheap
3. small   6. pretty   9. good

PRACTICE • *Make comparisons using the information given.*

> Jimmy weighs 150 pounds. Albert weighs 175 pounds.
> **Jimmy is lighter than Albert.**
> OR   **Albert is heavier than Jimmy.**

> Los Angeles doesn't get much rain. It rains a lot in San Francisco.
> **Los Angeles is drier than San Francisco.**
> OR   **San Francisco is wetter than Los Angeles.**

1. Johnnie can lift 100 pounds. Tino can lift 300 pounds.
2. Mr. Bascomb has a lot of money. Sam doesn't have very much.
3. Peter is five feet ten inches tall. Tino is six feet tall.
4. Peter's car is five years old. Tino's car is eight years old.
5. Peter's car can go 120 miles per hour. Tino's car can go 90 miles per hour.
6. Mrs. Golo weighs 125 pounds. Mrs. Brown weighs 155 pounds.
7. Johnnie takes a shower twice a day. Barney takes a shower twice a week.
8. Barbara is twenty-four years old. Tino is twenty-nine years old.
9. Wickam City is an average-sized town. Colterville is very small.

Rolls Royce

Honda

Nancy   Maria

Maria

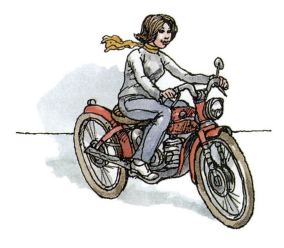

Nancy

Nancy

1. *Talk about the pictures.*
2. *Listen to the stories.*
3. *Answer the story questions.*

READING

1 The Rolls Royce is a very expensive car. It's much more expensive than a Honda. It's also more elegant and more comfortable. And, of course, a Rolls Royce is more powerful than a Honda. However, the Honda is a very popular car. It's more practical than a Rolls Royce. That's because it's smaller and more economical. It can travel twenty-five miles on a gallon of gas.

1. Which car is more expensive?
2. Which car is more elegant?
3. Is a Honda more comfortable than a Rolls Royce?
4. Which car is more powerful?
5. Which car is more practical?
6. Is a Honda more economical than a Rolls Royce?
7. How many miles can a Honda travel on a gallon of gas?

2 Nancy and Maria are both attractive women, but Maria is more elegant. She always wears beautiful clothes. Maria is also more artistic. She likes to paint and draw. On the other hand, Nancy is more adventurous. She flies an airplane and rides a motorcycle. She is also more athletic. She likes to play all kinds of sports.

1. Which of the two women is more elegant?
2. Which one is more artistic?
3. What does Maria like to do?
4. Is she more adventurous than Nancy?
5. Which woman is more athletic?
6. What does Nancy like to do?

LONG-WORD COMPARATIVE

Maria is more elegant than Nancy.
_____ artistic _____.
_____ popular _____.

WRITTEN EXERCISE • *Complete the sentences.*

Nancy is elegant, but Maria *is more elegant.*
Los Angeles is a beautiful city, but San Francisco *is more beautiful.*

1. Linda is athletic, but Jimmy _____.

2. Basketball is a popular sport, but football _____.

3. A Cadillac is expensive, but a Rolls Royce _____.

4. A Honda is economical, but a bicycle _____.

5. Barney is interesting, but Dr. Pasto _____.

6. Maria is energetic, but Nancy _____.

7. Mr. Bascomb is intelligent, but Dr. Pasto _____.

8. French is a difficult language, but German _____.

Listen and practice.

BARNEY: You know Sam Brown and Mr. Bascomb, don't you? They're good friends of yours, aren't they?

JACK: That's right. All of us belong to the Lions Club.

BARNEY: Do you think Mr. Bascomb is more successful than Sam?

JACK: That's a difficult question. Both men are good at their jobs.

BARNEY: Well, which one is more industrious?

JACK: I don't know. They both work very hard.

BARNEY: Do you think Sam is more popular than Mr. Bascomb?

JACK: Sure. Sam has more friends than anyone else in town.

BARNEY: But Mr. Bascomb is more generous than Sam, isn't he?

JACK: Only with his money.

BARNEY: You mean Sam is more generous with his time?

JACK: That's right. Last year he worked as a volunteer for the Fire Department.

BARNEY: That's interesting. Well, thanks for the information.

JACK: Wait a minute. Why are you asking all these questions?

BARNEY: So we can make a decision. We're trying to decide who will be the next Man of the Year.

GROUP WORK • *Ask and answer questions about these two men. Use the comparative form.*

> industrious
> A: **Who's more industrious, Sam or Mr. Bascomb?**
> B: **Mr. Bascomb is.**
> C: **You're right.**   OR   **You're wrong. Sam's more industrious.**

1. pleasant
2. successful
3. popular

4. energetic
5. relaxed
6. ambitious

7. sociable
8. intelligent
9. polite

WRITTEN EXERCISE • *Complete the sentences, using **more than** or **less than**.*

> Jimmy is (energetic) *more energetic* than Albert.
> Fred is (intelligent) *less intelligent* than Dr. Pasto.

1. A bicycle is (expensive) _____ than a car.

2. A Honda is (economical) _____ than a Rolls Royce.

3. It's (powerful) _____ than a Rolls Royce.

4. Mr. Bascomb is (industrious) _____ than most people.

5. Sam is (popular) _____ than anyone else in town.

6. Maria is (athletic) _____ than Nancy.

7. Life in the country is (peaceful) _____ than in the city.

8. Brasília is (modern) _____ than the average city.

9. Nancy Paine is (famous) _____ than Sophia Loren.

Last Saturday the Browns drove out to see the farm. Mr. Fix was standing in front of the farmhouse when they arrived.

"This is the place," he said. "You're really in the country now." He smiled as the Browns got out of their car and walked over to him. Mabel spoke first. "It's a long way from the city," she said. "It's farther than I thought."

"It's more peaceful that way," said Mr. Fix. "Just smell the air. It's cleaner here than in the city. And the farmhouse is very attractive, don't you think?"

"It's older and smaller than in the pictures," said Mabel. "And the barn doesn't look very solid."

"The house needs a paint job," said Sam. "And the gate is broken."

"You can fix it, Sam. That will be good exercise for you," said Mr. Fix.

"You said there was a stream, Mr. Fix. Where is it?"

"Well, this is the dry season," he explained. "It isn't very big this time of year."

"I can't even see it," said Jimmy. "And those fruit trees don't look very healthy."

"They just need a little water," said Mr. Fix.

"That horse is in pretty bad shape," said Sam. "He looked better in the picture."

"He just needs a little exercise," said Mr. Fix.

"I'm sorry, Mr. Fix," said Sam. "This farm is much worse than I expected. I was hoping for something better and less expensive."

"OK," said Mr. Fix, throwing his hands up in the air. "I give up." He was in a bad mood and left in a hurry. But when he got in the car and turned the key, nothing happened. "Oh no," he said. "I didn't get enough gas. The tank is empty."

Sam looked at him severely. "You can start walking, Mr. Fix."

"Why do you say that, Sam?"

"Because we're a long way from town and it's later than you think. Besides," he said, smiling, "it will be good exercise for you."

STORY QUESTIONS

1. Where did the Browns go last Saturday?
2. Who was standing in front of the farmhouse when they arrived?
3. Did the house look the same as in the pictures?
4. What did the house need?
5. What was wrong with the gate?
6. What else was wrong with the property?
7. Did Sam decide to buy the farm?
8. Why did Sam refuse to give Mr. Fix a ride into town?
9. Do you think Sam did the right thing? Why?
10. What is your opinion of Sam?
11. What do you think of Mr. Fix?
12. Why is Mr. Fix a poor salesman?

FREE RESPONSE

1. Do you believe these people are telling the truth? Why or why not?
2. Do you think most salespeople are honest?
3. Did you ever have an experience with a dishonest salesperson? If so, what happened?

WRITTEN EXERCISE • *Listen to the speakers and describe the emotion or mood of each one. Use these adjectives: **bored, angry, sad, worried, happy, scared.***

1. Tino *is happy*.
2. Jenny _____
3. Johnnie _____
4. Mona _____
5. Mr. Farley _____
6. Betty _____

PAIR WORK • *Ask and answer questions about these people.*

1. Tino
   A: **Why is Tino happy?**
   B: **He's happy because it's a beautiful day.**
   OR **He's happy because he's with his girlfriend.**

GROUP WORK • *Each student says one of these sentences four times with a different emotion each time: **happy, sad, angry, bored.** Change the order of the emotions. The other students try to guess the emotions of each speaker.*

1. Look at that man over there.
2. Jack, what are you doing here?
3. Every day I get up and go to work.
4. Are we having meatballs for dinner?

ROLE PLAY • *Choose one of the situations in the pictures and make up a conversation. Role play the conversation before the class. Be emotional!*

Listen and read.

GROUP WORK 1 • *Why is Sandy unhappy with her job? Which one of her problems at work do you think is the worst? Discuss this problem and try to find a solution.*

Useful words: receptionist, bellboy, guests, housekeeper, boss, paycheck

GROUP WORK 2 • *Make a list of the problems you have at work. Which problem is the most common? Discuss it and try to find a solution. Tell the class.*

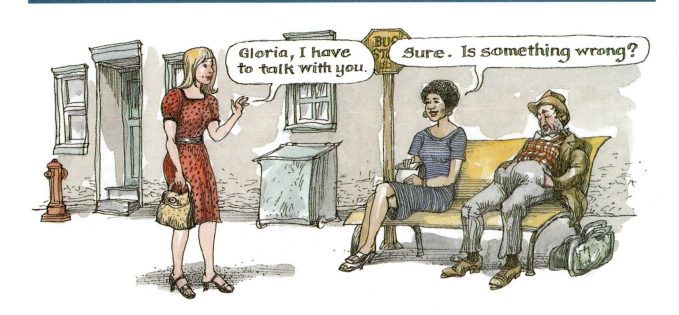

WRITTEN EXERCISE • *Complete the conversation between Sandy and Gloria. Use the comparative form of appropriate adjectives.*

1. **SANDY:**   I hate my job. It's so *boring*.

   GLORIA: I know what you mean. You'd like a _*more interesting*_ job.

2. **SANDY:**   My coworkers at the hotel aren't very *nice*.

   GLORIA: I'm sorry to hear that. You need to work with _*nicer*_ people.

3. **SANDY:**   I'm so tired. I have to work *long* hours.

   GLORIA: That's too bad. Ask your boss if you can work _____ hours.

4. **SANDY:**   My salary is very *low,* only a thousand dollars a month.

   GLORIA: Is that all? You need a job that pays a _____ salary.

5. **SANDY:**   I asked my boss for a raise, but he said no. He's very *stingy*.

   GLORIA: He should be _____.

6. **SANDY:**   He's always shouting at me. He's so *rude*.

   GLORIA: That's terrible! You need to work for someone who is _____.

7. **SANDY:**   I'm so *depressed*. I don't know what to do.

   GLORIA: Get another job. You'll be much _____.

8. **SANDY:**   You're right. But it's hard to find a *good* job.

   GLORIA: It's not impossible. I'm sure you can find a _____ job than the one you have now.

PAIR WORK • *Ask and answer the questions about your job.*

1. Do you like your job?
2. What are the good things about your job?
3. What are the bad things?
4. Do you like your boss? Why?
5. What are your coworkers like?
6. Are they the same age as you?

TALKING ABOUT JOBS

1. Do you think most people are happy with their jobs?
2. What are some typical complaints you hear when people talk about their jobs?
3. Do most employees like their bosses? Why?
4. What is your boss like? Is she a nice person? Does she ever shout at you?
5. Is your boss generous or stingy? Will she give you a raise?
6. What makes a good boss?
7. What makes a good employee?
8. Are you happy with your job? Why?
9. Would you like to have a different job? What would you really like to do?

ROLE PLAY

Student A doesn't like his job. Student B is his best friend.
Situation: Student A and Student B meet after work. Student A complains about his job.
Student B responds sympathetically.

Student A complains about:	Useful adjectives:	Student B's possible responses:
work	boring	I know what you mean.
boss	mean	That's too bad.
hours	long	I'm sorry to hear that.
coworkers	unfriendly	Really? I can't believe it.
salary	low	That's terrible. Why don't you quit?

COMPOSITION

1. Write about your job. What do you do? Are you happy with your job? Why?
2. Compare your hometown with the town you're living in now.

SHORT-WORD COMPARATIVE

He's	older stronger	than his friend.

He's	bigger fatter	than his friend.

She's	prettier friendlier	than her sister.

You have a	good typewriter. bad dictionary.

Irregular

It's	better worse	than mine.

LONG-WORD COMPARATIVE

Their car is	more expensive powerful	than ours.
	less economical practical	

Chapter

2

TOPICS

Personal experiences

Friends

Finding a job

Career counseling

GRAMMAR

Present perfect: regular and irregular verbs

Present perfect/past simple contrast

Present perfect with "for" and "since"

FUNCTIONS

Evaluating jobs

Applying for a job

Dr. Pasto has had a very interesting life. He has traveled around the world. He has visited the Great Wall of China. He has lived in Egypt and India. He has worked as a cook, lifeguard, photographer, and teacher.

The paragraph about Dr. Pasto is in the **present perfect.** We often use the present perfect to talk about personal experiences. We are not interested in when these things happened, but only in the fact that they have happened.

The present perfect is formed with the present tense of **to have** + past participle:
He **has traveled** around the world.   We **have visited** London.

With regular verbs, the past participle has the same form as the simple past:
worked   started   lived

PRACTICE • *Complete the sentences about the pictures using the present perfect.*

1. Dr. Pasto (travel) around the world.
   Dr. Pasto has traveled around the world.

2. Fred and Barney (shine) their shoes.
   Fred and Barney have shined their shoes.

3. Otis (paint) some beautiful pictures.

4. Sam and Mabel (visit) New York.

5. The Golos (finish) the housework.

6. Maria (live) in Paris.

7. Nick (work) hard today.

8. Jenny and Alice (learn) to play the piano.

PRACTICE • *Read the first sentence aloud. Then make a negative sentence about each picture.*

1. Gloria has washed the dishes.
But she hasn't washed the glasses.

2. Sam and Mabel have painted the bedroom.
But they haven't painted the bathroom.

3. Otis has repaired the roof.
_____ the door.

4. The Golos have cleaned the floor.
_____ the windows.

5. Barbara has sliced the pie.
_____ the cake.

6. Cathy has kissed Danny.
_____ Mike.

7. Jimmy and Linda have studied Spanish.
_____ French.

8. The girls have learned to play the piano.
_____ the violin.

It's nine o'clock Monday morning.

So far, Mrs. Golo
has taken a shower . . .

. . . gotten dressed

. . . eaten breakfast

. . . read the newspaper

and fed the cat.

Right now she's walking to the
bus stop. She's going to work.

We use the **present perfect** for past actions when there is a connection with the present. Mrs. Golo's actions began in the past and lead up to the present.

This page describes Mrs. Golo's actions using the past participle of irregular verbs: **taken   eaten   fed.**   There is a list of irregular verbs in the Appendix.

PRESENT PERFECT: Contractions

Mrs. Golo has eaten.	Mrs. Golo's eaten.	I have taken a shower.	I've taken a shower.
She _____.	She's _____.	You _____.	You've _____.
Barney _____.	Barney's _____.	We _____.	We've _____.
He _____.	He's _____.	They _____.	They've _____.

PRACTICE • *Make sentences for each picture using the present perfect.*

1. Mrs. Golo has eaten breakfast.
   We've eaten breakfast, too.

2. The Farleys have gone to work.
   Tino's gone to work, too.

3. Barney has gotten a haircut.
   I _____.

4. Sam and Mabel have seen The Statue of Liberty.
   Nancy _____.

5. Mr. Bascomb has made a lot of money.
   Our friends _____.

6. Suzi has read a lot of books.
   You _____.

7. Peter and Maria have had dinner at El Cholo.
   Anne _____.

8. Gloria has bought a lot of furniture.
   I _____.

9. Jimmy and Linda have been to Disneyland.
   Albert _____.

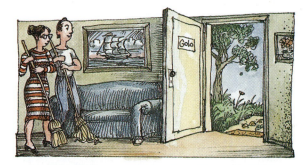

1. The Golos have done the housework.
   But they haven't done the yardwork.

2. Fred has slept on the sofa.
   But he hasn't slept on the floor.

3. Barney has driven a taxi.
   _____ a bus.

4. He's met Bonita Cantata.
   _____ Ula Hackey.

5. The Bascombs have been to Paris.
   _____ to London.

6. They've seen the Eiffel Tower.
   _____ the Tower of London.

7. Cathy has gone out with Danny.
   _____ Mike.

8. Willie has cut his hair.
   _____ his beard.

Listen and practice.

Maria and Dr. Pasto have known each other less than a year, but they have become good friends. They like many of the same things, including movies and travel.

DR. PASTO: Hi, Maria. Have you seen any good movies recently?

MARIA: Yes, I saw one last Friday.

DR. PASTO: What did you see?

MARIA: *An American in Paris* with Gene Kelly.

DR. PASTO: Oh, I know that one. I've seen it three times.

MARIA: Isn't it a wonderful picture? I liked it because the story took place in Paris.

DR. PASTO: Have you ever been to Paris?

MARIA: Yes, I studied medicine at the University of Paris. Didn't you know?

FREE RESPONSE • *Have you become friends with someone because you share similar interests? If so, who is this person and what are some things you both like?*

1. A: **Has Maria been to Paris?**
   B: **Yes, she has.**

2. A: **Have the Hambys paid their electric bill?**
   B: **No, they haven't.**

3. Have Sam and Mabel been to the market?

4. Has Mrs. Golo fed the cat?

5. Has Marty caught any fish?

6. Have Fred and Barney caught any fish?

7. Have Ed and Brutus eaten dinner?

8. Has Ed shaved recently?

1

2

1. *Talk about the pictures.*
2. *Listen to the stories.*
3. *Answer the story questions.*

READING

1 Mr. Bascomb has worked at City Bank for twenty years. He has been president for five years. City Bank has changed a lot since he became president. In the past, it was just an average bank. But now it's the number one bank in Wickam City. Mr. Bascomb has always worked very hard. He hasn't taken a vacation since 1985.

1. How long has Mr. Bascomb worked at City Bank?
2. How long has he been president?
3. How has City Bank changed since Mr. Bascomb became president?
4. Has Mr. Bascomb taken any vacations recently?

2 Barbara and Tino have gone out together for three years. Their relationship became serious a few months ago, and they decided to get married. Barbara and Tino have been engaged since last July. They are going to get married in a couple of weeks. Today they are looking for a wedding ring.

1. How long have Barbara and Tino gone out together?
2. When did they decide to get married?
3. How long have they been engaged?
4. When are they going to get married?
5. What are they doing today?

PRESENT PERFECT WITH **FOR**

They've gone out together for three years.

_____ a few months.

_____ several weeks.

_____ a long time.

PRACTICE • *Answer the questions using the present perfect with **for**.*

How long has Mr. Bascomb worked at City Bank?   (twenty years)
He's worked at City Bank for twenty years.

How long have Barbara and Tino been engaged?   (several weeks)
They've been engaged for several weeks.

1. How long have the Browns been in Wickam City?   (a long time)
2. How long have they lived in the same house?   (many years)
3. How long has Linda studied French?   (several months)
4. How long has Jimmy played football?   (a few years)
5. How long have they known Albert?   (a long time)
6. How long has Albert driven a car?   (one year)
7. How long has he had his new computer?   (a few weeks)
8. How long has Barbara worked at City Bank?   (a couple of years)
9. How long has Otis been an artist?   (ten years)

Listen and practice.

JIMMY: How long have you known Mr. Grubb?

SAM: I've known him for thirty years.

JIMMY: Then you've been friends since high school.

SAM: That's right, Jimmy.

LINDA: Has Dad always worn the same hat?

MABEL: Yes. He's had it since our marriage.

LINDA: Why doesn't he buy a new hat?

MABEL: He can't find a good one.

LINDA: How long has he looked?

MABEL: He's looked for months. It's hopeless.

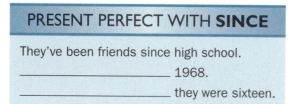

PRESENT PERFECT WITH **SINCE**

They've been friends since high school.

_____ 1968.

_____ they were sixteen.

PRACTICE 1 • _Answer the questions using the present perfect with_ **since.**

How long has Sam worn the same hat?   (his marriage)
He's worn the same hat <u>since his marriage</u>.

How long have Sam and Jack been friends?   (high school)
They've been friends <u>since high school</u>.

1. How long have Sam and Jack lived in Wickam City?   (their childhood)
2. How long have they belonged to the Lions Club?   (1984)
3. How long have the Browns had a garden?   (last spring)
4. How long has Linda studied music?   (high school)
5. How long has Otis painted pictures?   (he was a little boy)
6. How long has Jimmy known Albert?   (1993)
7. How long has Albert driven a car?   (last year)
8. How long have Barbara and Tino been engaged?   (last July)
9. How long have they played tennis together?   (last year)

PRESENT PERFECT WITH **FOR**

Sam's looked for a new hat for months.

_____ several weeks.

_____ a long time.

PRESENT PERFECT WITH **SINCE**

He's looked since April.

_____ last spring.

_____ his birthday.

PRACTICE 2 • _Answer the questions using the present perfect with_ **for** _or_ **since.**

How long has Barbara worked at the bank?   (a couple of years)
She's worked at the bank <u>for a couple of years</u>.

How long has Anne worked at the bank?   (last year)
She's worked at the bank <u>since last year</u>.

1. How long has Maria been a doctor?   (a few years)
2. How long has Albert had his new computer?   (last month)
3. How long has Mr. Bascomb worked at the bank?   (twenty years)
4. How long have the Golos lived in Wickam City?   (several years)
5. How long have they enjoyed classical music?   (they were teenagers)
6. How long has Johnnie owned the bookshop?   (a couple of years)
7. How long has he worn glasses?   (he was a little boy)
8. How long have your friends been in town?   (last month)
9. How long have they stayed at the same hotel?   (three weeks)

Elmer Coggins has been a farmer all his life. He has raised pigs and chickens for twenty years. He has grown a lot of corn, and his pigs have always been fat and healthy. However, this has been a bad year for Elmer. The weather has been dry for several weeks. It hasn't rained since March, and now it's June. Elmer is worried about his corn. Insects have destroyed part of his crop. Elmer hopes it will rain soon, so he won't lose the entire crop. He is also worried about his animals. His pigs are suffering and have lost a lot of weight. Elmer can't feed them well because he has very little corn. His chickens have done poorly, too. They have laid very few eggs recently.

"The situation hasn't been this bad since 1989," says Elmer. "That was the year our house burned down." He shakes his head and sighs. "My wife says we should sell the farm and move to the city. Sometimes I think she's right."

STORY QUESTIONS

1. How long has Elmer been a farmer?
2. How long has he raised pigs and chickens?
3. What kind of year has this been for Elmer?
4. How long has the weather been dry?
5. When was the last time it rained?
6. Why is Elmer worried about his corn?
7. Is he worried about his pigs and chickens? Why?
8. When was the last time Elmer had a terrible year? What happened?
9. What do you think Elmer should do about his situation? Why?
10. What do you think will happen?
11. How is Elmer's life different from yours?
12. Would you like to be a farmer? Why?

PRACTICE • *Read aloud these irregular verbs.*

be	been	go	gone	see	seen
buy	bought	lose	lost	speak	spoken
do	done	make	made	take	taken
eat	eaten	meet	met	wear	worn
forget	forgotten	read	read	write	written

WRITTEN EXERCISE • *Write four questions in the present perfect using four of the verbs above.*

Have you taken a vacation this year?
Have you lost anything recently?

PAIR WORK • *Ask your partner the questions you have written.*

A: **Have you taken a vacation this year?**
B: **Yes, I have. I went to New Orleans for the Jazz Festival.**
OR **No, I haven't. But I'm going to take a vacation soon.**

PRACTICE • *Complete the sentences using the present perfect with **since**.*

Otis and Gloria visited the museum last summer, **but they haven't visited the museum since.**

Fred called last month, **but he hasn't called since.**

1. Our friends were here last month, . . .
2. I spoke to them a few weeks ago, . . .
3. Jimmy and Linda watched television last weekend, . . .
4. Linda forgot to do her homework two weeks ago, . . .
5. They saw Albert last Sunday, . . .
6. It rained a couple of days ago, . . .
7. We traveled last year, . . .
8. Fred worked in 1990, . . .
9. My sister wrote to me last winter, . . .
10. Ed took a shower a week ago, . . .

PAIR WORK • *Ask and answer questions using the present perfect.*

> eat Japanese food
> A: **Have you ever eaten Japanese food?**
> B: **Yes, I have. I ate in a Japanese restaurant last month.**
>   OR   **No, I haven't. But I've eaten Chinese food.**

1. lose your keys
2. repair anything
3. visit a factory
4. go to the mountains
5. fish in the ocean
6. eat a hamburger
7. wear a cowboy hat
8. meet a famous person
9. see a play
10. write a poem
11. make a long-distance call
12. travel outside of the country

WRITTEN EXERCISE • *Complete the sentences using appropriate nouns. There can be more than one appropriate noun for each sentence.*

> I'm going to the _market_ to buy some milk.

1. The _____ is usually hot and dry at this time of year.

2. The people on our street are very friendly. We like all of our _____.

3. The _____ for this apartment is three hundred dollars a month.

4. All the _____ in the living room is new except the sofa.

5. I work very hard. I haven't taken a _____ since 1990.

6. I live a long _____ from my job.

7. My office is in a large _____ on State Street.

8. Joe's Cafe is usually empty. He doesn't have many _____.

9. People don't like to eat at Joe's because the _____ is terrible.

10. This morning Joe had an _____ and broke some plates.

11. Peter usually has cereal for _____ in the morning.

12. He brushes his teeth after every _____.

FREE RESPONSE

1. Do you like to shop? Where is your favorite place to buy clothes?
2. When was the last time you bought something on sale? What was it?
3. Do you like to eat out? Is there a good restaurant in your neighborhood?
4. Have you ever eaten Chinese food? What is your favorite kind of food?
5. Do you like to travel? Have you ever flown in an airplane? Where did you go?
6. Would you like to live in another city? Which one? Why?
7. What would you like to do this weekend? Do you have any plans?
8. Do you like to go to movies? Are there any good movies playing now?
9. What is your idea of a good time? What do you like to do for fun?

*********************CLASSIFIED ADS*********************

1	**DRIVER** 　　　SPEEDY CAB COMPANY Be Your Own Boss! Make up to $2,000/mo. No exp. nec. We will train. Must be 25 or older. Good driving record. Call Louie　555-0319
2	**RECEPTIONIST** Looking for friendly, enthusiastic person to answer calls and greet customers. Light typing. PT & FT positions available. $8.00/hr. Call Cornelius Rose　555-6925
3	**SALES** 　　　Make Big Money! Easily. Selling encyclopedias. No exp. nec. Will train right person. High comm. Earn $25–50k/yr. Must have positive attitude. Call: The Boss　555-7018

MANAGER TRAINEE 　　　$$$ BECOME RICH! $$$ *Men/women needed immediately *Once in a lifetime opportunity *Rapid advancement Our product is the best! Call Boston Blackie　555-2583	**4**
RESTAURANT Le Bistro is hiring waiters/waitresses. Work evenings/weekends PT & FT Min. 2 yrs. exp. Local ref. Must have good appearance. Call Pierre or Claudine　555-4510	**5**
TRAVEL 　　　See the World! Sunshine Travel is hiring tour guides. Must be friendly and have good appearance. Fluent in Spanish or French. Xlnt. salary and benefits. Call Janet　555-8931	**6**

Study the abbreviated words.

FT = full time
PT = part time
comm. = commission
xlnt. salary = excellent salary

$50k/yr. = fifty thousand dollars a year
no exp. nec. = no experience necessary
min. 2 yrs. exp. = minimum two years' experience
local ref. = local references

Study the following words and expressions.

Full time = 40 hours a week
Part time = less than 40 hours a week
Commission = a percentage of money from sales
Benefits = health insurance, paid vacations, etc.
Rapid advancement = you can move up quickly to a higher position
Local references = the people who recommend you for the job live in this area
Good appearance = you are neat and dress appropriately
Good driving record = you drive carefully and don't get any tickets
We will train = we will teach you how to do this job
Be your own boss = you make the decisions
Once in a lifetime opportunity = you seldom get an opportunity like this

PRACTICE • *Describe the jobs in the want ads.*

Number 1:　It's a job for a taxi driver. You can be your own boss and make up to two thousand
　　　　　dollars a month. You don't need any experience. The company will train you. You
　　　　　must be twenty-five or older and have a good driving record.

Listen and practice.

GLORIA: Are there any interesting jobs in the paper today?

SANDY: Here's one for a salesperson. It's a job selling encyclopedias.

GLORIA: What's the salary?

SANDY: I think it's commission only.

GLORIA: That's no good.

SANDY: There's another one here for a tour guide.

GLORIA: Sounds interesting.

SANDY: Yes, you get to travel and see the world.

GLORIA: Do they want someone with experience?

SANDY: It doesn't say.

GLORIA: Why don't you give them a call?

SANDY: I think I will.

GROUP WORK • *Talk about the jobs in the classified ads on page 34. Which job do you think is the best? Why?*

JANET: Sunshine Travel. May I help you?

SANDY: I'm calling about the job for a tour guide. Is it still open?

JANET: Yes, it is.

SANDY: What are the qualifications?

JANET: We're looking for someone with experience in the travel business. You must be good with people and speak at least one foreign language.

SANDY: How can I apply for the job?

JANET You have to come in, get an application, and make an appointment for an interview.

SANDY: Where are you located?

JANET: 537 Lime Street, downtown.

SANDY Thank you. I'll come tomorrow.

PAIR WORK • *Have similar conversations with a partner. Make a phone call to apply for one of the jobs on page 34. Ask about the salary and qualifications.*

PRACTICE • *This picture shows eight people at work. Give their occupations and tell what they're doing.*

> Number 1. **She's a nurse. She's caring for a patient.**

GROUP WORK • *Talk about the different occupations in the picture. Which one do you think is the most interesting? Why?*

ROLE PLAY

*Student A is having a problem choosing the right occupation. He/she goes to a career counselor (Student B) for help. The counselor asks some questions and then suggests an occupation. Take turns asking the following questions. You can answer **yes, no, very (good/well/much), not very (good/well/much),** or **more or less.***

1. Are you a good driver?
2. Do you know your way around town?
3. Are you friendly?
4. Do you work well with people?
5. Are you funny?
6. Do you like children?
7. Are you a good cook?
8. Do you want to be your own boss?
9. Are you good at repairing things?
10. Do you know a lot about cars?
11. Do you like office work?
12. Can you type?
13. Do you like to help others?
14. Are you good at caring for people?
15. Are you adventurous?
16. Do you want an exciting career?

GRAMMAR SUMMARY

PRESENT PERFECT Affirmative

He She	's (has)	taken a shower.
I You We They	've (have)	had breakfast. washed the dishes. cleaned the kitchen.

Negative

He She	hasn't (has not)	taken a shower.
I You We They	haven't (have not)	had breakfast. washed the dishes. cleaned the kitchen.

Interrogative

Has	he she	taken a shower?
Have	I you we they	had breakfast? washed the dishes? cleaned the kitchen?

Short Answers

Yes,	he she	has.	No,	he she	hasn't.
	I you we they	have.		I you we they	haven't.

Regular Verbs

He's (He has)	washed cleaned repaired painted	the car.

Irregular Verbs

She's (She has)	lost found taken forgotten	the money.

PRESENT PERFECT with FOR and SINCE

They've (They have)	worked lived	in Wickam City	for	several weeks. a few months. a long time.
			since	January. last year. 1975.

Negative

We haven't (We have not)	seen spoken to	Mr. Poole	for	a few weeks. a couple of months. a long time.
			since	last month. August. summer vacation.

Chapter 3

TOPICS
Eating out
Job interviews
Vacations

GRAMMAR
Infinitive of purpose
Present perfect with "just"
Present perfect with "already" and "yet"

FUNCTIONS
Stating purpose
Interviewing for a job
Asking for and giving information

1

2

1. *Talk about the pictures.*
2. *Listen to the stories.*
3. *Answer the story questions.*

READING

1 The Browns receive their mail every day at eleven o'clock. It's five minutes past eleven. The mail carrier has just delivered some letters. Mabel is going outside to get the mail. She is expecting a letter from her sister in Los Angeles.

1. When do the Browns receive their mail?
2. What time is it now?
3. What has the mail carrier just done?
4. Why is Mabel going outside?
5. What is she expecting?

2 Anne Jones and Johnnie Wilson both live in the same neighborhood. They have some friends in common, but they have never met each other before. Anne has just entered Johnnie's Bookshop for the first time. She wants to buy a Chinese cookbook. Johnnie has just seen her. He thinks she is very attractive.

1. What do Anne and Johnnie have in common?
2. Have they met each other before?
3. Has Anne been to Johnnie's Bookshop before?
4. What does she want to buy?
5. Has Johnnie seen Anne before?
6. What's his impression of her?

INFINITIVE OF PURPOSE

She's going outside to get the mail.

_____ to talk with the mail carrier.

_____ to feed the dog.

_____ to work in the garden.

WRITTEN EXERCISE • *Complete the sentences.*

Mabel is going outside *to get the mail.* _____

Anne has gone to the bookshop *to buy a cookbook.* _____

1. Albert and Linda are going to the library _____

2. Mrs. Golo has gone to the post office _____

3. Sam and Mabel have gone to the market _____

4. Nancy is going home _____

5. The boys have gone to the park _____

6. Jenny and Marty are going to the zoo _____

7. Barney is going to the barber shop _____

8. Fred has gone to the bank _____

9. I'm going to the drugstore _____

Listen and practice.

PRACTICE • *Make a sentence about each picture using the present perfect with **just**.*

1. Anne and Johnnie have just met each other.

2. Mabel _____

3. Peter _____

4. Mr. and Mrs. Bascomb _____

5. Barbara _____

6. Barney _____

7. Mr. and Mrs. Golo _____

8. Otis _____

1

2

1. Talk about the pictures.
2. Listen to the stories.
3. Answer the story questions.

READING

1 Barbara is getting ready to go out. She has a date with Tino tonight. She has already taken a bath and gotten dressed. Right now she is brushing her hair. Barbara hasn't put on her makeup yet. She is going to do that next.

1. Why is Barbara getting ready to go out?
2. Is she going to take a bath?
3. Has she already gotten dressed?
4. What's she doing now?
5. Has she put on her makeup yet?

2 Peter loves to travel and he has a great ambition: he wants to visit every part of the world. He has already been to Europe, Asia, and South America. But he hasn't been to Africa yet. He plans to go there next. He thinks it will be a great adventure.

1. What does Peter love to do?
2. What is his great ambition?
3. Has he already been to Europe?
4. Has he gone to Africa yet?
5. Does he plan to go there next?
6. What does he think a trip to Africa will be like?

PRESENT PERFECT WITH **ALREADY**	
Peter's already been to Europe.	They've already visited France.
He's _____.	You've _____.
Maria's _____.	We've _____.
She's _____.	I've _____.

PRACTICE • *Answer the questions using the present perfect with* **already**.

Is Barbara going to take a bath?
No, she's already taken a bath.

Are Mr. and Mrs. Bascomb going to read the newspaper?
No, they've already read the newspaper.

1. Are Jimmy and Linda going to have dinner?
2. Are they going to do their homework?
3. Are we going to study Chapter Two?
4. Is Barney going to fix up his taxi?
5. Is he going to pay back Mr. Bascomb?
6. Is Mrs. Golo going to feed the cat?
7. Are the Browns going to paint their house?
8. Are they going to plant some tomatoes?
9. Is Anne going to clean the windows?

Listen and practice.

BARBARA: Hello, Anne. How's everything?

ANNE: Fine. I met a nice man last week.

BARBARA: Have you gone out with him yet?

ANNE: Not yet. But he's already called me three times.

BARBARA: When will you see him again?

ANNE: Tomorrow. We're going to have dinner together. I can hardly wait.

FREE RESPONSE 1 • *Why is Anne so excited? Do you think it's OK for a woman to go out with a man she has just met?*

Listen and practice.

SAM: What would you like to do today?

MABEL: I'd like to go to the art museum.

SAM: Are you serious? We've already been there twice this month.

MABEL: But we haven't seen their new exhibition yet.

SAM: What exhibition?

MABEL: The one that started last Monday.

FREE RESPONSE 2 • *Have you been to a museum recently? If so, which museum did you go to? What did you see there?*

1. ☑ take out trash ☐ sweep sidewalk

A: Has Fred taken out the trash and swept the sidewalk?
B: He's taken out the trash, but he hasn't swept the sidewalk yet.

2. ☑ clean kitchen ☐ living room

A: Have Jimmy and Linda cleaned the kitchen and the living room?
B: They've cleaned the kitchen, but they haven't cleaned the living room yet.

3. ☑ repair roof ☐ door

4. ☑ feed dog ☐ cat

5. ☑ paint bedroom ☐ bathroom

6. ☑ wash car ☐ cut grass

7. ☑ wash dishes ☐ take out trash

8. ☑ clean windows ☐ make bed

Last night Anne and Johnnie had their first date. Johnnie wanted to do something special, so he invited Anne to have dinner at Captain Morgan's, a new restaurant named after the famous English pirate.

"Have you been here before?" asked Anne, as they entered the restaurant.

"No," said Johnnie. "But I hear it's very good. The seafood is supposed to be out of this world."

"Welcome to Captain Morgan's," said a young woman wearing a red dress. "I'm your hostess."

"Good evening," said Johnnie. "We'd like a table for two."

"Do you have reservations?"

"No, we don't," said Johnnie. "I didn't think it was necessary."

"It's all right—I'll find you a table. This way, please."

Anne and Johnnie followed the hostess to the back of the restaurant. "Here we are," she said, motioning to a small table in the corner.

"It's too noisy here," said Johnnie. "I can hear plates in the kitchen."

"Can't you give us another table?" asked Anne.

"I'm sorry. This is the only table that's free."

"Then we'll wait for another one," said Johnnie.

"OK," said the hostess, "but you'll have to wait at least an hour. There are several people ahead of you with reservations."

Johnnie was very disappointed. He turned to Anne. "What do you think?" he asked.

"This table is OK," said Anne. "We can sit here."

The hostess smiled. "I'll get the waiter," she said.

Anne and Johnnie were looking at the menu when they heard a deep voice.

"Good evening," said a big man dressed like a pirate. "I'm Blackbeard, your waiter."

"Good evening," said Johnnie.

"Have you decided yet?" asked Blackbeard.

"No, we don't understand the menu. Everything's in French."

"Of course," said Blackbeard. "French is the language of food."

"What do you recommend, Mr. Blackbeard?" asked Anne.

"The specialty of the house. Poisson cru à la mode."

"What's that?"

"Raw fish. You'll love it."

"OK," said Johnnie. "Bring us two of those."

"Very good," said Blackbeard.

"This place is really something," said Johnnie, looking around the restaurant. "I feel like I'm in a pirate ship. See the antique guns on the wall?"

Anne didn't say anything. Johnnie noticed that she was frowning. "What's the matter?" he asked.

"I don't like the way that bird is looking at me," said Anne, pointing to a huge parrot in a cage.

"He must like you, just like I do," said Johnnie, smiling.

"I'm not so sure," said Anne. "He looks dangerous to me."

"Don't worry. He can't do anything. He's just a dumb bird."

"Here's your dinner," said Blackbeard, setting two plates of fish on the table. "Bon appetit."

"Thank you," said Johnnie.

"Don't these fish look fresh?" said Anne, picking up her knife and fork.

"Yes, they look . . . alive!" said Johnnie. "My fish is moving!"

"So is mine," said Anne. "It's jumping on the plate."

"Waiter!" said Johnnie. "These fish are still alive. You served us live fish!"

"Of course," said Blackbeard calmly. "That's poisson cru à la mode."

"That's ridiculous," said Johnnie, getting up from the table.

"Where are you going?" asked Blackbeard.

"We're leaving!" said Anne. "This place is for the birds."

STORY QUESTIONS

1. Where did Anne and Johnnie go for dinner last night?
2. Did they have reservations?
3. Why didn't they like the table the hostess gave them?
4. Why did they decide to sit at that table anyway?
5. Who's Blackbeard? Describe him.
6. Why didn't Anne and Johnnie understand the menu?
7. What did Blackbeard recommend?
8. Why did Johnnie feel like he was in a pirate ship?
9. Why did Anne feel uncomfortable? Was it because of Blackbeard?
10. What did Johnnie say about the parrot?
11. Do you think the parrot was dangerous?
12. What did Blackbeard say when he served Anne and Johnnie their dinner?
13. Why were Anne and Johnnie surprised when they saw the fish?
14. What happened then? What did they do?

READER'S THEATER • *Four students take the roles of Anne, Johnnie, the hostess, and Blackbeard. A fifth student is the narrator. Read dramatically from the story.*

FREE RESPONSE

1. Do you like to eat out?
2. Have you ever been to a seafood restaurant?
3. Have you ever eaten raw fish? raw meat?
4. Would you like to have dinner at Captain Morgan's?
5. Can you recommend a good restaurant? Why is it good?
6. What is the most important thing in a restaurant—the food, the service, or the atmosphere?
7. Have you ever had an interesting experience in a restaurant? What happened?

PRACTICE 1 • *Make sentences using the present perfect with **already**.*

> Open the window!
> **I've already opened the window.**

1. Go to the market!	5. Clean the windows!	9. Close the gate!
2. Buy some eggs!	6. Feed the dog!	10. Lock the door!
3. Make some coffee!	7. Take out the trash!	11. Find the telephone book!
4. Wash the dishes!	8. Sweep the sidewalk!	12. Call the police!

PRACTICE 2 • *Answer the questions using the present perfect with **just**.*

> Is Nancy cleaning the bedroom?   Are Mr. and Mrs. Golo reading the newspaper?
> **No, she's just cleaned the bedroom.**   **No, they've just read the newspaper.**

1. Are Sam and Mabel having dinner?	6. Is Barbara buying a new dress?
2. Are they feeding the dog?	7. Is she paying the saleswoman?
3. Is Linda taking a shower?	8. Is Barney repairing his car?
4. Is Jimmy calling Albert?	9. Are the girls cleaning their room?
5. Are they doing their homework?	10. Are they making their beds?

WRITTEN EXERCISE • *Complete the sentences using the simple past or the present perfect.*

> Miss Hackey (be) _*has been*_ in town for a few days.
>
> She (arrive) _*arrived*_ at the Plaza Hotel Friday morning.

1. Nancy (study) _____ French since she was in high school.

2. She (visit) _____ Paris last summer.

3. Up to now, we (spend) _____ very little money on furniture.

4. We (buy) _____ a small table a few weeks ago for fifty dollars.

5. I (have) _____ some free time last night, so I (go) _____ to a movie.

6. I (see) _____ a lot of movies recently.

7. Yesterday Bob (invite) _____ Linda to a party.

8. She (be) _____ to three parties this month.

9. We (know) _____ Linda for a long time.

10. She looks much better since she (cut) _____ her hair.

PAIR WORK • *Find out what the other students in your class have done or haven't done so far today/this week/this month. Here are some suggestions. Add your own ideas.*

> Today: read the newspaper, open your mail, make the bed, eat lunch, see your friends, etc.
>
> A: **Have you read the newspaper today?**
> B: **Yes, I have. I read the newspaper this morning.**
>   OR **No, I haven't. I'm going to read the newspaper tonight.**
>
> This week: go to the market, do your laundry, clean your house, write a letter, see a movie, etc.
>
> This month: have a haircut, pay your bills, go to the bank, take a trip, meet any interesting people, etc.

FREE RESPONSE

1. Do you like the weather we're having today? Is this your favorite time of year?
2. Do you think today is a good day for a picnic?
3. Do you think it's more fun to have a picnic or eat in a restaurant?
4. Where did you have lunch yesterday? What did you eat?
5. What were you doing an hour ago? What were you doing at this time yesterday?
6. How long have you studied English? Have you studied any other languages?
7. How many books have you read this year? Which one was the best?
8. When was the last time you bought something? What was it?
9. What is the best thing that has happened to you recently?

Listen and practice.

Sandy Benton is having a job interview with Mr. Winkle, president of Sunshine Travel.

MR. WINKLE: Good morning, Miss Benton.

MISS BENTON: Good morning.

MR. WINKLE: So you want to be a tour manager?

MISS BENTON: That's right.

MR. WINKLE: Have you ever worked in the travel business?

MISS BENTON: No, but I've traveled to a lot of foreign countries. And I can speak three languages.

MR. WINKLE: That's good. What kind of work experience do you have?

MISS BENTON: Right now I'm working at the Regal Hotel as a receptionist. Before that, I was a waitress at the Magnolia Restaurant.

MR. WINKLE: Tell me more about yourself, Miss Benton. What are your strong points?

MISS BENTON: Well, I'm friendly. I like people. And I'm a hard worker.

MR. WINKLE: Why do you want to work for this company?

MISS BENTON: Sunshine Travel has a very good reputation. You're the best travel agency in town.

MR. WINKLE: Thank you. Do you have any questions, Miss Benton?

MISS BENTON: Yes, how much is the starting salary?

MR. WINKLE: Two thousand dollars a month, plus living expenses.

MISS BENTON: That sounds good.

MR. WINKLE: Yes, it's a good job. I'll look over your application and call you in a few days.

MISS BENTON: Thank you.

PAIR WORK • *Have a job interview with your partner. The interview can be for any job.*

EMPLOYER: Good morning, _____.

JOB APPLICANT: Good morning.

EMPLOYER: So you want to be a _____?

JOB APPLICANT: _____

EMPLOYER: What kind of work experience do you have?

JOB APPLICANT: _____

EMPLOYER: Tell me more about yourself. What are your strong points?

JOB APPLICANT: _____

EMPLOYER: Why do you want to work for this company?

JOB APPLICANT: _____

EMPLOYER: Do you have any questions?

JOB APPLICANT: _____

EMPLOYER: I'll look over your application and call you in a few days.

JOB APPLICANT: _____

Listen and practice.

FREE RESPONSE • *Do you think Gladys will get the job? Why? What did she do wrong?*

GROUP WORK • *Look at the answers Gladys gave Mr. Winkle. See if you can give better answers to his questions. Make a list of your group's best answers and read them to the class.*

Yosemite National Park is one of the most famous parks in the United States. It has beautiful mountains, rivers, and forests. You can go fishing, swimming, camping, hiking, and horseback riding. It's a wonderful place for a vacation.

1. Have you ever been to a national park?
2. Have you ever gone camping? fishing? horseback riding?
3. What is the most famous national park in your country?
4. What kind of things can you do there?

TALKING ABOUT VACATIONS

1. Where did you go on your last vacation?
2. How did you get there?
3. Who did you go with?
4. What did you do?
5. Where did you stay?
6. How was the food?
7. Did you buy anything?
8. Did you meet any interesting people?
9. What was the best part of your vacation?

GROUP WORK • *In groups of three talk about the best vacation you've ever had.*

COMPOSITION •

1. Write about your favorite vacation. Where did you go? What did you do?
2. Write about a memorable experience you had in a restaurant.

INFINITIVE OF PURPOSE

| She's going to the post office. | She's going | to get a package.
to buy some stamps.
to send some letters. |

| She's going to the post office | to get a package.
to buy some stamps.
to send some letters. |

PAST SIMPLE

| He
She
I
You
We
They | took a shower
ate breakfast
called Maria | a few minutes ago. |

PRESENT PERFECT with JUST

| He
She | 's
(has) | | taken a shower. |
| I
You
We
They | 've
(have) | just | eaten breakfast.
called Maria. |

PRESENT PERFECT with ALREADY
Affirmative

| He
She | 's
(has) | | met Peter. |
| I
You
We
They | 've
(have) | already | talked to him.
seen his car. |

PRESENT PERFECT with YET
Negative

| He
She | hasn't
(has not) | met Peter | |
| I
You
We
They | haven't
(have not) | talked to him
seen his car | yet. |

PRESENT PERFECT with YET
Interrogative

| Has | he
she | met Peter | |
| Have | I
you
we
they | talked to him
seen his car | yet? |

Short Answers

| Yes, | he
she | has. | No, | he
she | hasn't. |
| | I
you
we
they | have. | | I
you
we
they | haven't. |

Chapter

TOPICS
Food
Good deeds
Sports
Clothes

GRAMMAR
Review

FUNCTIONS
Giving opinions
Agreeing and disagreeing
Talking about changes
Solving problems
Making complaints
Buying clothes
Asking permission
Congratulating

On his way home from school, Jimmy Brown often stops at Brady's Newsstand on Main Street. Jimmy loves to look at magazines, and Brady's has the best selection in town. Sometimes Jimmy spends the whole afternoon reading about sports, movies, and pop music. Mr. Brady, the owner of the newsstand, is a very kind man. He doesn't mind if Jimmy looks at the magazines, as long as he puts them back in the right place.

At the moment, Jimmy is reading an article about famous actors of the silent era. Mr. Brady looks over Jimmy's shoulder and smiles. "We had a lot of great actors in those days," he says. "But if you ask me, Charlie Chaplin was the greatest."

"I've never seen any of his pictures," says Jimmy. "What's so great about him?"

"He was a master of comedy," says Mr. Brady. "Charlie Chaplin was one of the funniest men who ever lived."

"He looks funny in this photograph," says Jimmy. "Did he always dress like a bum?"

"Yeah, in most of his pictures he wore an old coat and baggy pants. Everyone called him the little tramp."

"I don't think I'd like to be a tramp," says Jimmy. "But I would like to travel and have adventures, like Charlie Chaplin did."

"There's plenty of time for that," says Mr. Brady. "Hey kid, will you watch the stand for a minute? I'm going across the street to get a cup of coffee."

"Sure, Mr. Brady. I'll be happy to."

As Jimmy is looking at magazines, he hears the roar of a motorcycle. He turns around and sees a gray-haired woman on a huge, black Honda. She jumps off the bike and takes a magazine off the rack.

"Where's Mr. Brady?" she asks.

"He went across the street. He'll be back soon."

"I can't wait," says the woman. "I'm in a hurry."

"Is there something you want to buy?" asks Jimmy.

"Yes, I want to get this magazine," she says.

"You can pay me. I'll give him the money."

The woman observes Jimmy carefully. "You look like an honest boy," she says. "I guess I can trust you." She takes out two dollars and hands the money to Jimmy. Then she jumps on her motorcycle and takes off. "Make sure he gets it," she yells, roaring down the street.

"Don't worry," says Jimmy.

A minute later, Mr. Brady comes back holding a cup of coffee. "Thanks for watching the store, kid."

"Sure, anytime, Mr. Brady. Oh, I sold a magazine while you were gone. Here's the money."

"Good kid," says Mr. Brady. He puts the money in the cash register and sits down in his chair. Jimmy watches Mr. Brady as he drinks his coffee. His hands shake a little and he gets some coffee on his shirt. "Darn it," he says. "I have to be more careful." He takes out a handkerchief and starts cleaning his shirt. Jimmy notices the wrinkles on Mr. Brady's hands, and the lines on his face. He looks at his snow-white hair.

"Mr. Brady," says Jimmy, "can I ask you something?"

"Sure, kid."

"What was it like when you were young?"

Mr. Brady finishes his coffee and throws the cup in the trash.

"You really want to know?"

Jimmy nods his head.

"Well, of course, everything was different then. Music, clothes, entertainment . . . "

"What was the music like?" asks Jimmy.

"It was terrific. When I was your age, we listened to big band music by Glenn Miller and Duke Ellington. You have your rock 'n' roll, which is OK, but the music we had was much more romantic. We liked to dance cheek-to-cheek."

"Were you a good dancer, Mr. Brady?"

"I don't like to brag, kid, but I was one of the best. All the girls loved to dance with me. I was the king of the Starlight Ballroom."

"The Starlight Ballroom? Where's that?"

"They closed it down twenty years ago," says Mr. Brady, sadly.

"Oh, that was dumb," says Jimmy.

"I hope I can make a trip across the ocean someday," says Jimmy. "Have you ever been to a foreign country, Mr. Brady?"

"Sure, I've been all over the world. Rio, Hong Kong, Cairo. . . . I've seen everything and done it all."

"Gee, I've never been out of Wickam City," says Jimmy.

"Don't worry, you'll get your chance. You have a spirit of adventure, and that's what counts."

"Thanks, Mr. Brady. Well, I'd better go now. It's getting late."

"So long, kid."

"Bye, Mr. Brady."

"That's life," says Mr. Brady. "Times change."

"Do you think times were better then or now?" asks Jimmy.

"Well, when I was young, life was slower and less complicated," says Mr. Brady. "We had fewer problems with noise, pollution, and crime. But some things are better now, like medicine and transportation. People live longer and travel faster nowadays. I remember it took Lindbergh thirty-three hours to fly across the Atlantic in 1927, and everybody thought it was fantastic. They gave him a hero's welcome when he landed in France. Today, you can cross the same ocean in less than four hours, and nobody thinks anything of it."

STORY QUESTIONS

1. Why does Jimmy go to Brady's Newsstand?
2. What does Jimmy like to read about?
3. What is Mr. Brady's opinion of Charlie Chaplin?
4. How did Charlie Chaplin dress?
5. Why does Mr. Brady ask Jimmy to watch the newsstand?
6. Who arrives at the newsstand after Mr. Brady leaves?
7. What does the woman want?
8. What happens when Mr. Brady starts drinking his coffee?
9. How old do you think Mr. Brady is?
10. What kind of music was popular when Mr. Brady was young?
11. Why does Mr. Brady like big band music better than rock?
12. Was Mr. Brady a good dancer? Where did he like to dance?
13. What happened to the Starlight Ballroom?
14. How was life different when Mr. Brady was young?
15. What things are better today?
16. How long did it take Lindbergh to cross the Atlantic?
17. Where did he land?
18. How long does it take to make the same trip today?
19. What does Jimmy hope to do some day?
20. Does Jimmy have a spirit of adventure? What about you?

FREE RESPONSE • *Mike Brady has been around for a long time, and he has opinions on everything. He likes to talk about how things have changed since he was a young man. Do you agree or disagree with his comments? Why?*

1. "When I was young, there was much less crime. The streets were safer, and we never locked our doors."
2. "People are less friendly nowadays. Most people don't even know their neighbors."
3. "Kids are smarter today. They know much more than the kids of my generation."
4. "The family is less important today. People only care about their careers and making money."
5. "Life is much easier nowadays. Machines do all the work."
6. "People are healthier nowadays. They eat better and live longer."

GROUP WORK • *Talk about your city. How has it changed in the last ten years? List three things that have gotten better and three things that have gotten worse. How have these things gotten better or worse?*

CLASS ACTIVITY • *Talk about the picture. What are the people doing?*

FREE RESPONSE

1. Have you ever eaten at a sidewalk cafe? Are sidewalk cafes popular in your country?
2. What's the difference between a cafeteria and a restaurant? Do you pay tips in a cafeteria?
3. When was the last time you had a picnic? Where was it?
4. What kind of things can you cook on a barbecue?
5. What kind of food can you buy from a catering truck?
6. Do you sometimes take your lunch to work or school?
7. Do you like to cook? What kind of dishes can you make?
8. What are the advantages of eating at home? Eating out?
9. What do you think of American food? What is typical American food?

GROUP WORK • *Talk about the food in your country. What are some typical dishes? What kind of food do you like best?*

GROUP WORK • *Discuss the problems these people are having at work. Try to find solutions.*

ROLE PLAY • *Choose one of these situations and make up a conversation. Role play the conversation before the class.*

FREE RESPONSE

Why are these people complaining? What do you think they are saying?

When was the last time you complained about something? What were you upset about? Tell what happened.

Describe what is happening in the pictures below.

When was the last time you saw someone do a "good deed"? Have you done any good deeds recently? Do you think most people try to help others, or do they just mind their own business?

FREE RESPONSE • *Answer the questions about yesterday.*

1. What did you do yesterday?
2. Did you drive or take the bus anywhere?
3. Did you meet anyone interesting? Where? How?
4. Did you buy anything? What? Where?
5. How much money did you spend?
6. How many phone calls did you make?
7. Who did you talk with? What did you talk about?
8. What did you wear yesterday?
9. Did you enjoy the weather? Why?
10. What was the best or worst thing that happened to you yesterday?

GROUP WORK • *Talk about yesterday or last weekend. What did you do?*

Student A: **I went to the park last Sunday.**

The other students ask questions like these:

What park did you go to?	How was the weather?
Who did you go with?	Did you have a good time?

WRITTEN EXERCISE • *Complete the sentences using **someone, something, somewhere, anyone, anything,** and **anywhere.***

Albert doesn't know *anything* about sports.

Linda can't go *anywhere* tonight. She has to stay home.

Can I use your phone? I have to call *someone* .

1. I'm hungry. I want _____ to eat.

2. There isn't _____ in the refrigerator.

3. Go to Mom's Cafe. You can't find better food _____.

4. I hear footsteps. I think there's _____ in the hall.

5. The hall is empty. I don't see _____.

6. Come here. There's _____ I have to tell you.

7. This isn't a good place to talk. Let's go _____ else.

8. I can't go _____. I don't have my car keys.

9. Don't worry. I won't tell _____ that you lost your keys.

10. The keys were in the desk a little while ago. _____ took them.

11. Don't look at me. I didn't do _____.

12. Tell the truth. Did you take the keys and hide them _____?

WRITTEN EXERCISE • *Linda is shopping for a pair of jeans. Complete the conversation between Linda and the salesman using these sentences:*

They're a size smaller.
I like the ones with the stripes.
Well, how do they fit?
I'd like to buy a pair of jeans.
You can try them on in the dressing room.

These are much better.
What style do you like?
They're a little too big.
Can I help you?

PAIR WORK • *Have similar conversations. One student is the salesperson in a clothing store. The other student is a customer who wants to buy a pair of jeans, a shirt, or a dress.*

PRACTICE • *Disagree with the statements using the short-answer form.*

> Mike Brady is rich. **No, he isn't.**
> He doesn't have to work. **Yes, he does.**

1. Captain Morgan's is a good restaurant.
2. It isn't expensive.
3. Barbara drives to work.
4. She doesn't take the bus.
5. Jack has worked hard this year.
6. He hasn't taken a vacation.
7. The weather was good last month.
8. It didn't rain much.
9. We can go to the movies tonight.
10. We don't have to study.
11. Linda stayed home last night.
12. She didn't go out with her friends.

WRITTEN EXERCISE • *Add an explanation to each of these remarks.*

> Hurry up! *We're late.*
> OR *The show starts in five minutes.*
> I admire your sister. *She's a beautiful person.*
> OR *She always tries to help people.*

1. He's a lucky man. _____
2. I'm worried. _____
3. Can you loan me some money? _____
4. Don't turn off the radio! _____
5. How can you eat that food? _____
6. Speak louder. _____
7. Peter can't go to work today. _____
8. I had a terrible time last night. _____
9. Diane isn't talking to her boyfriend. _____
10. Can I use your umbrella? _____
11. I don't like to take the bus. _____
12. Nobody eats at Joe's Cafe. _____

WRITTEN EXERCISE • *Write an appropriate sentence for each picture using these sentences.*

Television soap operas are very popular.
Some people live to work.
Baseball is the national pastime.
Coffee is the favorite drink.
Women live longer than men.

There are many races and nationalities.
Young people enjoy rock music.
The average family has two children.
People eat a lot of junk food.

1. *There are many races and nationalities.*

2. _____

3. _____

4. _____

5. _____

6. _____

7. _____

8. _____

9. _____

FREE RESPONSE

1. Are there many races and nationalities in your country? Do most people speak the same language? How many people speak English in your country?
2. What is the national pastime in your country? What's your favorite pastime? Do you like sports?
3. What is junk food? Do you sometimes eat junk food? Can you get a hamburger and french fries in your country?
4. Do you enjoy soap operas? Are soap operas popular in your country? What is your favorite TV program?
5. Is rock music popular in your country? Can you name any rock bands? What kind of music do you like best?
6. What is the most popular drink in your country? How much coffee do people drink? What do people drink with meals? What's your favorite drink?
7. How big is the average family in your country? How many people are there in your family? Do you think it's better to have a large family or a small family? Give reasons for your answer.
8. What is a "workaholic"? Why do some people work so hard? Do you think most people live to work or live to play?
9. Do women live longer than men in your country? Why do you think women live longer in the United States? What is necessary for a person to live a long, happy life?

WRITTEN EXERCISE • *Complete the sentences using **everyone, everything, everywhere, no one, nothing,** and **nowhere.***

All the employees are having lunch. There's ___*no one*___ in the office.

I can't find my dictionary. I've looked for it ___*everywhere*___.

Fred is bored. He has ___*nothing*___ to do.

1. The refrigerator is empty. There's _____ in it.

2. We're all broke. _____ has any money.

3. I have to find an apartment right away. I have _____ to stay.

4. If you need help, go to Dr. Pasto. He helps _____.

5. I called him last night, but there was _____ home.

6. While Mabel was sick, Sam took care of the family. He did _____.

7. Mabel is fine now. There's _____ wrong with her.

8. My uncle loves to travel. He's been _____.

9. There's _____ more exciting than New York City. It's a great place.

10. Baseball is America's favorite sport. _____ likes baseball.

11. I've never seen so many tourists. They're _____.

12. That's life. You can't have _____.

 *Listen and practice.*

ED: Do you mind if I turn on the radio?

JOHNNIE: Yes, I do. Please don't turn it on.

PAIR WORK • *Have similar conversations. Student A asks for permission to do something. Student B can either give or deny permission.*

A: Do you mind if I _____?

B: Yes I do. Please don't _____.
OR No, I don't. (It's OK.) (Go ahead.)

Use these ideas for your conversations:

1. open the window?
2. eat your sandwich?
3. read the newspaper?
4. use your comb?
5. use the mirror?
6. look at the map?
7. take off my shoes?
8. sit in the back seat?
9. play my bongos?

WRITTEN EXERCISE • *Americans often use shortened questions in conversation. Write the complete question form after the shortened questions.*

Working hard? *Are you working hard?*

Want a cup of coffee? *Do you want a cup of coffee?*

Heard the news? *Have you heard the news?*

1. Having a good time? _____

2. Come here often? _____

3. Hungry? _____

4. Had lunch yet? _____

5. Ever been to Joe's Cafe? _____

6. Anything wrong? _____

7. Need some help? _____

8. Going home? _____

9. Want a ride? _____

CONVERSATION

🔊 *Listen and practice.*

SANDY: Gloria, I got the job!

GLORIA: Congratulations!

SANDY: Thank you.

GLORIA: When do you start?

SANDY: Next week.

GLORIA: You must be happy.

SANDY: Yes, I'm very happy.

PAIR WORK • *Have similar conversations. Use your imagination.*

1. Congratulations!
   _____ name?
   How old _____?

2. Congratulations!
   _____ name?
   How _____ meet her?

3. Congratulations!
   When _____?
   How much _____?

4. Congratulations!
   How much _____?
   How _____ spend it?

5. Congratulations!
   How _____ do it?
   How _____ feel?

6. Congratulations!
   Where _____?
   What _____ do now?

Review • Chapter 4 **69**

FREE RESPONSE

1. What's the first thing you do when you get up in the morning?
2. What's the last thing you do before you go to bed at night?
3. What are your plans for the weekend?
4. Can you recommend an interesting movie or book? Why do you think it's good?
5. When was the last time you bought an article of clothing? What was it?
6. Have you ever loaned money to someone? Did you get the money back?
7. Have you ever borrowed money? What did you need the money for?
8. When was the last time you forgot something? What was it?
9. When was the last time you helped someone? What did you do?

ONE STEP FURTHER

TALKING ABOUT SPORTS

1. What's your favorite sport?
2. What's the most popular sport in your country?
3. What's your favorite team?
4. Who's your favorite player?
5. What's your opinion of professional sports? athletes?
6. What sports do you play?
7. What are the benefits of playing a sport?

COMPOSITION

1. Write about your favorite sport.
2. How are Americans similar to or different from people in your country?
   Compare work, play, family life, etc.
3. Write about a good deed you did or that someone else did.

1. This has been a wet year.

   We've had _____ rain.

   a. many   c. a few
   b. little   d. a lot of

2. Jack is lazy. He works only

   _____ hours a day.

   a. a few   c. much
   b. a lot of d. many

3. You're going to be a good dancer.

   You just need _____ practice.

   a. much   c. a little
   b. many   d. a few

4. We don't know _____ people
   on our street.

   a. much   c. each
   b. many   d. a little

5. I can't think when there's _____
   noise.

   a. too much c. too little
   b. too many d. too few

6. Linda is talking to Albert _____
   the phone.

   a. in   c. at
   b. on   d. with

7. Let's have lunch _____ Mom's Cafe.

   a. for   c. at
   b. to   d. on

8. Peter is taking Maria _____ the
   movies.

   a. in   c. at
   b. for   d. to

9. Wickam City is ten miles _____ the
   ocean.

   a. to   c. for
   b. at   d. from

10. Mr. Bascomb is president _____ a
    large bank.

    a. of   c. with
    b. for   d. from

11. Peter's car is in good condition.

    He takes good care of _____.

    a. him   c. them
    b. her   d. it

12. We're having a problem. Can you

    help _____?

    a. it   c. us
    b. we   d. them

13. Where are the boys? Are _____ at
    the park?

    a. they   c. their
    b. them   d. there

14. Sam is happy _____ he has a
    good job and a nice family.

    a. although c. so
    b. because d. but

15. I was hungry, _____ I made a
    sandwich.

    a. although c. so
    b. because d. but

16. We called your house last night,

    but there was _____ home.

    a. anyone   c. no person
    b. none   d. nobody

17. The umbrella is _____ in the
    living room.

    a. somewhere c. everywhere
    b. anywhere d. where

18. There's _____ wrong with the
    television. It works perfectly.

    a. something c. nothing
    b. anything d. everything

19. You can't use that typewriter.

    It's _____.

    a. broke   c. cheap
    b. broken   d. old

20. I can't talk to you now. I'm _____.

    a. lonely   c. happy
    b. bored   d. busy

21. Gloria works during the day and studies at _____.
    a. night   c. afternoon
    b. morning   d. weekend

22. Joe's Cafe is usually empty. He doesn't have many _____.
    a. customers   c. eaters
    b. buyers   d. shoppers

23. Sandy usually has cereal for _____ in the morning.
    a. snack   c. lunch
    b. breakfast   d. dinner

24. I want every apple in the box. Give me _____ of them.
    a. most   c. none
    b. some   d. all

25. Both of those boys are smart. _____ of them is dumb.
    a. None   c. All
    b. Neither   d. One

26. The students are doing _____ lessons.
    a. there   c. their
    b. yours   d. theirs

27. Those people are friends of _____.
    a. we   c. our
    b. us   d. ours

28. My dictionary is _____ than yours.
    a. good   c. better
    b. more good   d. more better

29. Mrs. Golo is a bad dancer, but her husband is even _____.
    a. worse   c. badly
    b. more worse   d. more bad

30. You look thirsty. _____ I make some lemonade?
    a. Would   c. Will
    b. Shall   d. Must

31. Nancy is very intelligent. She _____ speak several languages.
    a. can   c. will
    b. must   d. would

32. Jack is always at the library. He _____ read a lot.
    a. will   c. must
    b. can   d. would

33. Dr. Pasto is coming. He _____ be here in a few minutes.
    a. must   c. can
    b. would   d. will

34. Jimmy is seventeen. He isn't _____ to vote.
    a. so old   c. enough old
    b. very old   d. old enough

35. Mabel is _____ to make dinner.
    a. very tired   c. so tired
    b. too tired   d. tired enough

36. We always dress _____ on cold days.
    a. slowly   c. warmly
    b. poorly   d. badly

37. If you want to be successful, you have to work _____.
    a. hard   c. good
    b. hardly   d. intelligent

38. Mr. Poole walks _____ when he's in a hurry.
    a. quick   c. slow
    b. fast   d. energetic

39. The boys often _____ football in the park.
    a. play   c. are playing
    b. plays   d. were playing

40. Barbara was sitting in a cafe when she _____ Tino.
    a. meets   c. has met
    b. is meeting   d. met

41. Jack _____ dinner yet.

    a. doesn't eat   c. hasn't eaten
    b. don't eat   d. didn't eat

42. Gloria _____ some furniture last week.

    a. buy   c. pay
    b. bought   d. paid

43. We _____ cards when our friends called.

    a. was playing   c. are playing
    b. were playing   d. have played

44. Otis _____ at the same address since 1990.

    a. lives   c. lived
    b. is living   d. has lived

45. You haven't cleaned the kitchen, _____?

    a. have you   c. haven't you
    b. you have   d. you haven't

46. Jimmy likes sports, _____?

    a. does he   c. doesn't he
    b. he does   d. he doesn't

47. Did Maria go to a movie with Peter?

    Yes, she _____.

    a. go   c. went
    b. did go   d. did

48. Are the Browns going to buy a new TV?

    Yes, they _____.

    a. are   c. do
    b. buy   d. have

49. Have you seen Fred?

    Yes, I _____ him last week.

    a. ran over   c. looked up to
    b. ran into   d. stood up for

50. If it's too hot in here, you can _____ your jacket.

    a. turn off   c. take off
    b. get off   d. put off

Chapter

5

TOPICS
People
Transportation

GRAMMAR
Superlative

FUNCTIONS
Describing people and things
Describing outstanding features
Asking for and giving directions
Giving reasons

1

2

1. *Talk about the pictures.*
2. *Listen to the stories.*
3. *Answer the story questions.*

1 Barbara and Tino got married today. They had the biggest wedding of the year. Everyone was there. Barbara wore a lovely white wedding dress. She was the prettiest girl at the wedding. And Tino was a very handsome groom. Today they were the happiest couple in Wickam City.

1. Who got married today?
2. Did they have a big wedding?
3. Who was the prettiest girl at the wedding?
4. What did she wear?
5. Were Barbara and Tino very happy today?

2 Sam Brown is the best shoe repairman in Wickam City. His prices are the lowest and his service is the fastest. People always compliment Sam on his fine work. In fact, Sam gets the most compliments and the fewest complaints of any shoe repairman in town.

1. Who is the best shoe repairman in Wickam City?
2. Does anyone have lower prices than Sam?
3. Does anyone have faster service?
4. Does Sam get many compliments?
5. What about complaints?

SHORT-WORD SUPERLATIVE

Sam is the nicest shoe repairman in town.

_____ fastest _____.

_____ busiest _____.

_____ friendliest _____.

PRACTICE • *Make sentences using the superlative form.*

Barbara and Tino/happy couple/Wickam City
Barbara and Tino are the happiest couple in Wickam City.

Sam/fast shoe repairman/town
Sam is the fastest shoe repairman in town.

Slim Skinner/thin boy/his school
Slim Skinner is the thinnest boy in his school.

1. Fred/lazy man/town
2. Mrs. Watkins/old woman/Wickam City
3. Linda and Jane/smart girls/their class
4. Mr. and Mrs. Bascomb/rich couple/town
5. Mr. Twaddle/short man/Wickam City
6. Alaska/big state/the United States
7. Mount Everest/high mountain/the world
8. The Nile/long river/the world
9. The Sears Tower/tall building/the world

Listen and practice.

SALESMAN: Can I help you, ma'am?

MRS. BROWN: Yes. I'm looking for a bright summer dress.

SALESMAN: How about this one?

MRS. BROWN: It isn't very bright.

SALESMAN: It's the brightest dress we have.

MRS. BROWN: It looks expensive.

SALESMAN: It's the cheapest dress in the store.

MRS. BROWN: Have you got it in a larger size?

SALESMAN: It's the largest dress they make.

MRS. BROWN: OK. I'll take it.

PAIR WORK • *Have conversations like the one on page 77.*

A: Can I help you?

B: Yes. I'm looking for a _____ .

A: How about this one?

B: It isn't very _____ .

A: It's the _____ we have.

1. bright dress

2. wide belt

3. pretty blouse

4. nice shirt

5. large hat

6. warm coat

7. soft pillow

8. big handbag

9. strong suitcase

GROUP WORK • *Talk about your favorite clothes. Ask and answer these questions.*

- What is your favorite article of clothing?
- Why is it special?
- How long have you had it?
- When do you like to wear it?

1. *Talk about the pictures.*
2. *Listen to the stories.*
3. *Answer the story questions.*

Mr. Bascomb, Dr. Pasto, and Mayor Connors are three of the most important men in Wickam City. Mayor Connors is the most powerful of the three. As the head of city government, he makes decisions that affect the lives of everyone in Wickam City. Frank Connors has already served four terms as mayor and plans to retire at the end of this year.

Dr. Pasto is the most intelligent and most sophisticated of the three men. He knows a lot about the world from personal experience, while the other two men have never lived outside of Wickam City.

Mr. Bascomb is the most ambitious of the three men. He is president of the biggest bank in town, and would like to be the next mayor of Wickam City. He wants to be mayor so he can bring more business to the city. He thinks that only the mayor has enough power and influence to do it.

1. Who are three of the most important men in Wickam City?
2. Who is the most powerful of the three? Why?
3. Is he going to serve another term as mayor?
4. Who is the most intelligent of the three?
5. Is he also the most sophisticated? Why?
6. Who is the most ambitious of the three men?
7. Why does Mr. Bascomb want to be the next mayor of Wickam City?

LONG-WORD SUPERLATIVE

Dr. Pasto is the most sophisticated man in Wickam City.

_____ intelligent _____.

_____ interesting _____.

_____ unusual _____.

PRACTICE • *Make sentences using the superlative form.*

Mr. Bascomb/ambitious man/town
Mr. Bascomb is the most ambitious man in town.

Paris/beautiful city/world
Paris is the most beautiful city in the world.

1. Mayor Connors/powerful man/Wickam City
2. Ula Hackey/famous person/Wickam City
3. Nancy/adventurous woman/Wickam City
4. Jimmy/intelligent boy/his class
5. Mabel/energetic person/her family
6. Sam/popular man/town
7. Jack/dangerous driver/town
8. Mr. Bascomb/successful man/town
9. New York/important city/the United States

Listen and practice.

Suzi Suzuki is asking Jack some questions about Dr. Pasto for a feature story she's writing for the Wickam Daily News.

SUZI: How long have you known Dr. Pasto?

JACK: About five years.

SUZI: What's the first thing about him that impressed you?

JACK: His intelligence. He's the most intelligent man I've ever met.

SUZI: He's an expert on anthropology, isn't he?

JACK: Yes, in fact, he's one of the most respected men in his profession. He's written several books about primitive societies.

SUZI: Is it true that he once lived with the dangerous Yahyah tribe on the Passion Islands?

JACK: That's right. He even went hunting and fishing with them.

SUZI: He's quite adventurous, isn't he?

JACK: No doubt about it. He's the most adventurous man I've ever known.

SUZI: And the most impressive, it seems. Now I'd like to talk to Dr. Pasto himself. Do you know where I can find him?

JACK: Yes, he's probably at home chasing butterflies right now.

ROLE PLAY • *Student A is a reporter for a newspaper. Student B is Dr. Pasto. The reporter interviews Dr. Pasto for an article in the newspaper. Use some of the questions in the dialogue above and make up your own questions.*

WRITTEN EXERCISE • *Complete the following sentences.*

Mr. Bascomb is the (rich) _____*richest*_____ man in town.

Sam is the (popular) *most popular* man in town.

1. Tino is the (strong) _____ man I've ever met.

2. Dr. Pasto has the (beautiful) _____ house I've ever seen.

3. City Bank is the (successful) _____ bank in Wickam City.

4. Mr. Bascomb is the (busy) _____ man I've ever known.

5. He's the (ambitious) _____ man in town.

6. Mrs. Golo is the (bad) _____ dancer I've ever seen.

7. She has the (ugly) _____ cat in the neighborhood.

8. Simon is the (unusual) _____ person I've ever met.

9. Linda is the (good) _____ student in her class.

10. Otis is the (original) _____ artist in Wickam City.

11. Los Angeles is the (big) _____ city in California.

12. English is the (important) _____ language in the world.

PRACTICE • *Make sentences using the superlative form.*

Mr. Bascomb is more ambitious than anyone else in Wickam City.
He's the <u>most ambitious</u> man in town.

Mabel is very friendly and talks to everyone she meets.
She's the <u>friendliest</u> person in town.

1. Dr. Pasto is more sophisticated than anyone I've ever met.
2. Nancy has more energy than anyone I've ever known.
3. Tino has a lot of friends, a good job, and a beautiful wife.
4. Fred never works.
5. Mrs. Watkins is 112 years old.
6. Mr. Stilt is eight feet tall.
7. Mrs. Hamby weighs 300 pounds.
8. Mr. Bascomb has more money than anyone else in Wickam City.
9. Sam has more friends than anyone else in Wickam City.

Jimmy Brown plays basketball for the Tigers. He is captain of the team. Some of the boys are taller than Jimmy, but he is the most valuable player. He is the quickest and he scores the most points. All the boys like Jimmy; he is the most popular player on the team. He is also the most competitive; he hates to lose.

Right now, the Tigers are practicing for today's big game. They need a lot of practice. They have won only two games this year, and they have lost nine. However, last year the Tigers were even worse than this year. They didn't win any games. They were the worst team in the league.

In a few minutes, the Tigers will play the Wildcats. The coach of the Tigers is giving his players some words of encouragement.

"The Wildcats are bigger, faster, and stronger than you are," he says. "But don't worry. You have a better coach."

STORY QUESTIONS

1. What team does Jimmy play for?
2. Is he the tallest player on the team?
3. Why is Jimmy the most valuable player?
4. What are the Tigers doing now?
5. Why do they need so much practice?
6. Do you think the Tigers have a good coach? Why?
7. Who will the Tigers play today?
8. Which team do you think will win the game? Why?

Anne
28 years old
5'5" tall

Barbara
24 years old
5'4" tall

Maria
27 years old
5'7" tall

GROUP WORK • *Ask and answer questions about the three women. Use the superlative form.*

friendly
A: **Which one is the friendliest?**
B: **Anne is.**
C: **You're right.**   OR   **I disagree. I think Barbara is the friendliest.**

1. tall	4. old	7. relaxed
2. short	5. happy	8. elegant
3. young	6. busy	9. interesting

FREE RESPONSE

1. What is the largest river in your country?
2. What is the highest mountain?
3. What is the biggest lake?
4. What is the most important city?
5. What is the most important industry?
6. What is the best newspaper?
7. What is the most popular magazine?
8. What is the most popular television program?
9. What is the most popular sport?
10. Who is the most famous athlete?
11. Who is the best singer?
12. Who is the most important person?

• *Nancy is having a party. Do you know the names of her guests? Number one is Peter.*

CONVERSATION • *Listen and practice.*

LISA: Who's that man over there?

NANCY: That's Peter.

LISA: He's very popular, isn't he?

NANCY: Yes. He's the most popular man I know.

PAIR WORK • *Have similar conversations.*

A: Who's that man/woman over there?

B: That's _____.

A: He's/She's very _____, isn't he/she?

B: Yes. He's/She's the _____ man/woman/person I know.

   OR   I don't think so.

Here are some adjectives you can use to describe the guests.

shy	popular
rich	nervous
happy	beautiful
strong	intelligent
friendly	good-looking

1 Los Angeles

2 Paris

3 Peking

4 San Francisco

5 Rio de Janeiro

6 Rome

7 New York

8 Venice

9 Jaipur

PRACTICE • *Describe the different means of transportation using the superlative form of these adjectives: **fast, slow, safe, cheap, expensive, popular, enjoyable, famous, exciting, comfortable.** Use the adjective you think is the most appropriate for each kind of transportation.*

1. Los Angeles
   In Los Angeles, the most popular means of transportation is the car.

2. Paris
   In Paris, the fastest means of transportation is the Metro.

3. Peking
4. San Francisco
5. Rio de Janeiro

6. Rome
7. New York

8. Venice
9. Jaipur

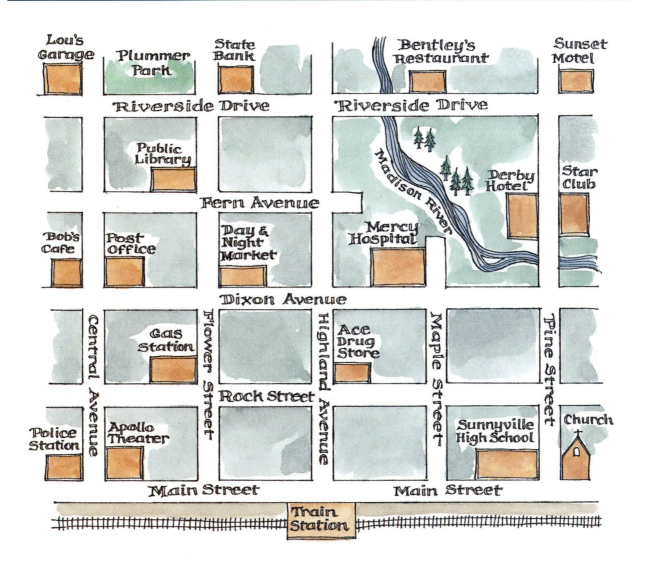

PAIR WORK • *You're at the train station. Ask for and give directions.*

A: Excuse me. Is there a market nearby?

B: Yes. There's one on Dixon Avenue.

A: Can you tell me how to get there?

B: Sure. Go (down) one block to Flower Street.

A: Flower Street?

B: Yes. Then turn right and go (up) two blocks. You'll see it on the corner.

A: Thank you.

B: You're welcome.

A: Excuse me. I'm looking for the Star Club.

B: It's on Pine Street across from the Derby Hotel.

A: Where's that?

B: Go (down) two blocks to Pine Street. Turn left and go straight (up). It's on the other side of the river.

A: Thanks

B: Sure.

1. library
2. Mercy Hospital
3. Bob's Cafe
4. bank
5. Derby Hotel
6. Plummer Park
7. gas station
8. Bentley's Restaurant
9. Apollo Theater
10. Sunset Motel
11. post office
12. drugstore

I admire Ula Hackey for her **talent**. She's a great actress. She's made many wonderful movies.

I admire Dr. Pasto for his **bravery**. He's faced danger many times in his life. He's not afraid of anything.

I admire my mother for her **kindness and generosity**. She always tries to help people. Everyone loves her.

ADMIRABLE QUALITIES • *Match each word below with its definition.*

bravery	the ability to learn or understand
generosity	being faithful to one's country, friends, or ideals
honesty	not afraid, without fear in the face of danger
humor	a superior ability in an art
intelligence	willing to give or share
kindness	the ability to appreciate or express what is funny
loyalty	truthful, unwilling to lie or steal
talent	the habit of being sympathetic or gentle

TALKING ABOUT PEOPLE

1. Who do you admire?
2. Why do you admire this person?
3. Has this person had an influence on your life? How?

GROUP WORK • *Discuss people you admire with other students in your class. Who is your choice for "Man of the Year" or "Woman of the Year"? Give reasons for your choice.*

COMPOSITION • *Write about a person you admire. What special qualities does this person have? What has he or she done that is outstanding?*

SHORT-WORD COMPARATIVE and SUPERLATIVE

old strong	older stronger	oldest strongest		big fat	bigger fatter	biggest fattest

			Irregular		
pretty friendly	prettier friendlier	prettiest friendliest	good bad	better worse	best worst

He's the	oldest biggest friendliest best	student in his class.

LONG-WORD COMPARATIVE and SUPERLATIVE

popular elegant	more popular elegant	most popular elegant

She's the	most beautiful sophisticated	woman in town.

GO + -ING FORM

They	go	fishing hunting swimming sailing	all the time.

Chapter 6

TOPICS
Marriage
Crime

GRAMMAR
Used to
Adjective + infinitive
Who/that/which in defining relative clauses

FUNCTIONS
Describing past habits
Clarifying/making specific
Telling a story
Giving excuses
Reporting a crime

THEN

NOW

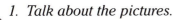
1. *Talk about the pictures.*
2. *Listen to the story.*
3. *Answer the story questions.*

READING

Tino's life has changed a lot since his marriage. He used to live in a small apartment on Oak Street, but now he lives in a house with Barbara. He used to go out with his friends at night, but now he stays home with his wife. They usually watch television together or play cards. Tino used to sleep late and never got up before ten o'clock in the morning. Now he gets up at seven and drives Barbara to work. He used to have his meals at the restaurant, but now he eats at home. For better or worse, life is not the same for Tino.

1. Now that Tino is married, his life isn't the same, is it?
2. Where did Tino use to live?
3. Where does he live now?
4. What did Tino use to do at night?
5. What does he do now?
6. Did Tino use to get up early in the morning?
7. What time does he get up now?
8. Where did Tino use to eat?
9. Where does he eat now?
10. Do you think Tino's life has gotten better or worse since his marriage?

USED TO
Tino used to live in a small apartment, but he doesn't anymore.
_____ sleep late in the morning, _____.
_____ meet his friends at night, _____.
_____ eat at the restaurant, _____.

PRACTICE • *Make sentences with **used to** and **anymore**.*

Tino/lived on Oak Street
Tino used to live on Oak Street, but he doesn't anymore.

We/watch television
We used to watch television, but we don't anymore.

1. Tino/sleep late in the morning
2. Barbara/take the bus to work
3. They/like rock music
4. Fred/work at the garage
5. Mr. and Mrs. Hamby/travel a lot
6. Barney/eat at Joe's Cafe
7. Ula Hackey/live in Hollywood
8. She/wear expensive clothes
9. Sam and Jack/play basketball

Listen and practice.

ANNE: Hello, Barbara. What are you making?

BARBARA: Lasagna. It's for our dinner tonight.

ANNE: Oh, really? You never used to make Italian food.

BARBARA: Things are different now that I'm married. Besides, it's fun to cook.

ANNE: What else is new in your life?

BARBARA: Well, I used to take the bus to work, but now I get a ride with Tino.

ANNE: Is Tino a good driver?

BARBARA: I think so. He used to drive very fast, but he's more careful now. There are a lot of children in this neighborhood, you know.

ANNE: Do you and Tino plan to have many children?

BARBARA: Only two. It's expensive to have a big family nowadays.

ANNE: You're right. Well, I have to go now. Give my regards to Tino when you see him.

BARBARA: I'll be glad to. Goodbye, Anne.

FREE RESPONSE • *How has Barbara's life changed now that she's married to Tino? Do you think Barbara enjoys being married? Why?*

Listen and repeat.

PAIR WORK • *Have similar conversations.*

1. Barbara speaks Italian now.　2. Barbara makes pasta now.　3. Barbara likes opera now.

4. Tino goes home after work now.　5. Tino eats at home now.　6. Tino stays home and watches TV now.

TALKING ABOUT MARRIAGE

1. How does marriage change people?
2. What do you think a wife's role should be in a marriage?
3. What do you think a husband's role should be?
4. Who do you think should be the head of the house—the wife or the husband?
5. What are the advantages of being married?
6. What are the disadvantages?
7. Do you think marriage is more advantageous for men or women? Why?

GROUP WORK • *What do you think is necessary for a happy marriage? Make a list of your ideas and share them with the class.*

1. *Talk about the pictures.*
2. *Listen to the story.*
3. *Answer the story questions.*

Last night a burglar broke into Dr. Pasto's house and stole most of his butterfly collection. The burglar took all the rare butterflies that were in the cabinet, while leaving the ordinary butterflies that were on the wall. As he was going out the window, the burglar made a noise and Dr. Pasto woke up. Dr. Pasto looked outside and saw the burglar, who was running across the front yard. He didn't get a good look at him, but noticed that he was wearing a black patch over one eye. Dr. Pasto picked up the phone that was next to his bed and called the police. The police captain asked for a description of the man who stole the butterflies. Dr. Pasto thought for a moment and said, "The man who broke into my house had a patch over one eye. I'm sorry, Captain, that's all I can tell you." "Don't worry," said the police captain. "I promise to find the man who took your butterflies."

1. What happened last night?
2. Which butterflies did the burglar take?
3. What happened as the burglar was leaving the house?
4. Did Dr. Pasto see the burglar?
5. What was he doing when Dr. Pasto saw him?
6. What did Dr. Pasto notice about the man?
7. Who did Dr. Pasto call?
8. Did he use the phone that was in the living room?
9. What did the police captain ask for?
10. What did Dr. Pasto say about the man who broke into his house?
11. What did the police captain promise to do?

THE RELATIVE PRONOUN **THAT**

He picked up the phone that was in the bedroom.
_____ that was next to his bed.
_____ that was on the table.
_____ that was by the window.

PRACTICE • *Combine the sentences using **that**.*

Dr. Pasto picked up the phone. It was next to his bed.
Dr. Pasto picked up the phone that was next to his bed.

The burglar took the butterflies. They were in the cabinet.
The burglar took the butterflies that were in the cabinet.

1. He left the ordinary butterflies. They were on the wall.
2. I painted the table. It was in the garage.
3. We looked at the magazines. They were on the table.
4. She picked up the newspaper. It was on the floor.
5. He signed the forms. They were on his desk.
6. They read the telegram. It arrived this morning.
7. I took the apples. They were in the bag.
8. She wore the dress. It belonged to her mother.
9. He bought the suit. It was on sale.

Listen and practice.

BARNEY: What do you think about the butterfly theft?

FRED: I don't understand it. Butterflies are easy to catch. Anyone who steals them must be crazy.

BARNEY: Not necessarily. Dr. Pasto had some butterflies that were very valuable.

FRED: How much do you think his collection is worth?

BARNEY: It's hard to say. Perhaps five thousand dollars for the whole collection.

FRED: Do you think the burglar will try to sell the butterflies?

BARNEY: Yes, but not in Wickam City. He's probably gone to a large city to sell them.

FRED: Wait a minute. The burglar was wearing a black patch, wasn't he?

BARNEY: That's right. Why?

FRED: I used to know a man who wore a black patch. Maybe he's the man who took the butterflies.

BARNEY: I doubt it. The police found the patch the burglar was wearing. It was a disguise.

FRED: Well, he must be very clever. I hope the police catch him.

FREE RESPONSE • *Do you think the police will catch the burglar? Who do you think is smarter, the burglar or the police?*

THE RELATIVE PRONOUN **WHO**

The police are looking for the man who robbed Dr. Pasto.

_____ who broke into his house.

_____ who opened his cabinet.

_____ who stole his butterflies.

PRACTICE 1 • *Combine the following pairs of sentences using the relative pronoun* ***who.***

Dr. Pasto saw the man. He took the butterflies.
Dr. Pasto saw the man who took the butterflies.

I know the girls. They work at the library.
I know the girls who work at the library.

1. We know the woman. She lives across the street.
2. She kissed the man. He found her keys.
3. They talked to the policeman. He was standing on the corner.
4. I watched the children. They were playing in the park.
5. We heard the woman. She was singing in the shower.
6. They helped the man. He was looking for a job.
7. He thanked the people. They took care of his dog.
8. I met the girl. She worked at the bank.
9. We admire the boys. They play on the football team.

PRACTICE 2 • *Combine the following pairs of sentences using the relative pronouns* ***who*** *and* ***that.***

That's the man. He stole the butterflies.
That's the man who stole the butterflies.

Here's the patch. It belonged to the thief.
Here's the patch that belonged to the thief.

1. That's the woman. She lives across the street.
2. Those are the men. They work at the post office.
3. Here are the letters. They came this morning.
4. This is the book. It belonged to my father.
5. There's the computer. It was in your office.
6. Those are the boys. They helped me last night.
7. That's the girl. She lost her umbrella.
8. Here's the telegram. It arrived this afternoon.
9. There's the man. He delivered the telegram.

Yesterday the police caught the man who stole Dr. Pasto's butterflies. His name is Alexander Hampton. He's a clever thief who used to work in a circus. For years he was known as Alexander the Great, Master of Disguise. He was using one of his disguises, a black patch, when he stole Dr. Pasto's butterflies. The police captured him after he tried to sell the valuable collection to a large museum in San Francisco.

When Alexander went to the museum, he showed the butterflies to Sy Polanski, the museum director. As Mr. Polanski was examining the collection, a look of surprise came over his face. He thought the butterflies looked very familiar. The museum director suspected that Alexander was not the real owner of the butterflies and decided to ask him a few questions.

"These butterflies are very rare," he said. "Where did you get them?"

"They belonged to my father," said Alexander, who was an experienced liar. "He gave them to me as a present."

"I see," said Mr. Polanski. "And where did your father get them?"

"My father used to travel a lot," said Alexander. "He got those butterflies when he was in South America."

"That's very interesting," said Mr. Polanski. He noted that most of the butterflies were African butterflies, not South American butterflies. "How much do you want for your collection?"

"Five thousand dollars," said Alexander. "A very good price for such a valuable collection."

"Yes, that sounds like a reasonable amount," said Mr. Polanski. He made out a check for five thousand dollars and handed it to Alexander, who was smiling. Alexander thanked the museum director and left the room.

Mr. Polanski immediately called the police and told them about his meeting with the butterfly thief. He gave them a full description of Alexander and said that Alexander was going to the Federal Bank to cash the check. When Alexander arrived at the bank, the police were there waiting for him. They arrested him and took off his disguise.

"How did you know it was me?" asked Alexander.

"The museum director is an old friend of Dr. Pasto's, the man you robbed," said the Captain. "He recognized the butterflies you showed him."

STORY QUESTIONS

1. Who did the police catch yesterday?
2. Where did Alexander use to work?
3. What disguise was Alexander wearing when he stole Dr. Pasto's butterflies?
4. Who did Alexander show the butterflies to when he went to the museum?
5. Why didn't Mr. Polanski think that Alexander was the real owner of the butterflies?
6. Where did Alexander say he got the butterflies?
7. How much did he want for the collection?
8. Did Mr. Polanski give him the money in cash?
9. What did Mr. Polanski do after Alexander left the room?
10. What did the police do when Alexander arrived at the bank?

WRITTEN EXERCISE • *Combine the sentences.*

A woman helped me. I thanked her.

I thanked the woman who helped me.

Some boys are following us. Do you know them?

Do you know the boys who are following us?

1. A man repaired our television. We paid him.

_____

2. Some girls took your magazines. I saw them.

_____

3. A woman owns that company. We know her.

_____

4. A police officer found her handbag. She thanked him.

_____

5. Some tourists arrived at the airport. I met them.

_____

6. A tall blond woman works at the bank. Do you know her?

_____

7. An old man was here a little while ago. Did you see him?

_____

8. Some people were talking in the hall. I heard them.

_____

FREE RESPONSE

1. What is your favorite kind of entertainment?
2. Where do you go when you want to have a good time?
3. Do you like to go downtown? What's the best way to get there from your home?
4. What are some of the most important streets in this city?
5. What kind of transportation do you normally use?
6. What are the advantages of driving a car?
7. What are the advantages of taking the bus?
8. Do you have any complaints about the public transportation in this city?
9. What do you think are some of the most serious problems in this city?
10. What are some things you like about this city?

GROUP WORK • *What happened to Anne this morning? Tell Anne's story in your own words. One student describes the first picture, another student describes the second picture, and so on. For example:*

A: **This morning Anne woke up at seven o'clock. The sun was shining through the window.**

Listen and repeat.

ANNE JONES:	I'm sorry I'm late.
MR. BASCOMB:	What happened?
ANNE JONES:	*I got stuck in a traffic jam.*
MR. BASCOMB:	I've heard that one before.

PAIR WORK • *Have similar conversations with a partner.*

1. I had an accident.

2. I missed the bus.

3. I got a flat tire.

4. I didn't feel well.

5. I forgot something.

6. My car broke down.

7. My alarm clock didn't work.

8. I got an important telephone call.

9. I ran into an old friend.

GROUP WORK • *Talk about a time when you were late. What happened?*

ROLE PLAY 1

Student A plays Dr. Pasto. Student B plays the police captain.
Situation: Dr. Pasto calls the police to report a robbery. The police captain asks Dr. Pasto some questions. He needs the following information:

1. the time of the robbery
2. the location of the robbery
3. a description of the stolen property
4. a description of the thief
5. how the robbery happened

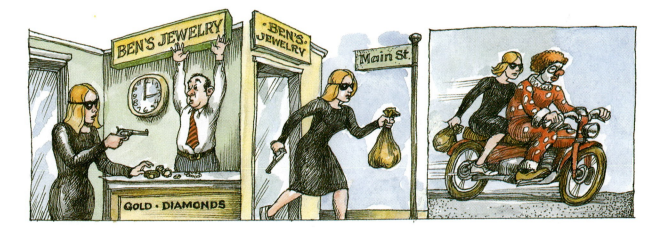

ROLE PLAY 2

Student A plays the manager of a jewelry store. Student B plays the police captain.
Situation: The manager calls the police to report the robbery of his jewelry store. The police captain asks for information about the robbery.

ROLE PLAY 3

Student A plays Joe. Student B plays the bandit.

Situation: The bandit tries to rob Joe's Cafe. Joe says there is no money in the cash register. He tells the bandit about his personal problems: he has no customers, his business is a failure, his wife is leaving him. The bandit doesn't care about Joe's problems. She's hungry. She wants something to eat.

TALKING ABOUT CRIME

1. Are there many robberies or holdups where you live?
2. What are some other common crimes?
3. Why is there so much crime nowadays?
4. Is crime a major problem where you live?
5. Is it safe to walk the streets at night?
6. Does your city have a good police department?
7. How is it possible to reduce crime? Do you have any suggestions?

GROUP WORK • Discuss ways to reduce crime and make a list of possible solutions.

COMPOSITION

1. Write about a famous robbery or holdup. What did the robbers take? When and where did it happen? Did the police catch the robbers? How?
2. Describe your dream house. What color is it? How many rooms does it have? What is the furniture like? Does it have a balcony? a fireplace? Is there a garden?

GRAMMAR SUMMARY

USED TO Affirmative

He She I You We They	used to	watch television every day. play basketball after school. take the bus in the morning.

Negative

He She I You We They	didn't use to never used to	get up early. drink coffee. work hard.

Interrogative

Did you	use to	walk to work?		Yes, I did.		No, I didn't.

DEFINING RELATIVE CLAUSES   People as Subject

He's the man We know the woman Those are the boys	who/that	owns the bookshop. lives across the street. found my dog.

Things as Subject

She picked up the cards It was my umbrella Here's the telegram	that/which	were on the floor. was in the car. arrived in the morning.

DEFINING RELATIVE CLAUSES   People as Object (Contact Clauses)

The man The people That's the girl	(who/that)	I used to know worked in a circus. you met last night are good friends of mine. we saw at the park yesterday.

Things as Object (Contact Clauses)

The dress The paintings That's the movie	(that/which)	she bought was on sale. we saw were very interesting. Jimmy was talking about.

Chapter

7

TOPICS
Clothes
Cars
Pets

GRAMMAR
As + adjective + as
As + adverb + as
Comparison of adverbs
Could
So/neither

FUNCTIONS
Comparing
Persuading
Making suggestions
Storytelling

CONVERSATION

Listen and practice.

SANDY: How do you like my new hat, Gloria?

GLORIA: It's very nice. Just like the one Maria has.

SANDY: Are you sure her hat is the same as mine?

GLORIA: Absolutely. I was with her when she got it.

SANDY: She doesn't have a blouse like this one, does she?

GLORIA: No, but I bought a blouse this morning, and it's the same as yours.

PRACTICE • *Compare the articles of clothing in the pictures. Are they the same or different?*

1. Sandy's hat   Maria's hat

Sandy's hat is the same as Maria's.

2. your tie   my tie

Your tie is different from mine.

3. Tino's shirt   Peter's shirt

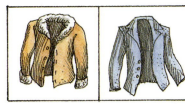

4. his coat   your coat

5. her dress   my dress

6. Sandy's blouse Gloria's blouse

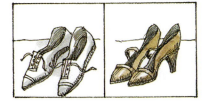

7. your shoes   her shoes

8. Sam's belt   Jack's belt

9. my sweater   his sweater

Listen and practice.

BARNEY: Look. Maxie Gold is going to fight the Champ tonight. I'll bet he wins.

JACK: I don't know, Barney. The Champ is very strong.

BARNEY: So is Maxie. He's as strong as the Champ.

JACK: But he isn't as clever. He doesn't have as much experience as the Champ does.

BARNEY: You're right. He hasn't had as many fights. But I still think Maxie is going to win.

JACK: Why?

BARNEY: Because the Champ is getting old. He isn't as fast as he used to be.

PAIR WORK • *Add sentences using **as + adjective + as.***

A: The Champ is very strong.
B: So is Maxie. **He's as strong as the Champ (is).**

A: Jimmy is very popular.
B: So is Linda. **She's as popular as he is.**

A: They're very energetic.
B: So are we. **We're as energetic as they are.**

1. A: Peter is very sophisticated.
   B: So is Maria.

2. A: They're very intelligent.
   B: So are we.

3. A: Mabel is very friendly.
   B: So is Sam.

4. A: They're very generous.
   B: So are you.

5. A: We're very hungry.
   B: So is Albert.

6. A: He's very tired.
   B: So am I.

7. A: Our friends are very lucky.
   B: So are we.

8. A: We're very successful.
   B: So are they.

9. A: Barney is very nice.
   B: So is Nancy.

10. A: They're very smart.
    B: So are you.

CONVERSATION

Listen and practice.

JOHNNIE: Tino plays tennis very well, doesn't he?

ANNE: So does Barbara. She plays as well as he does.

JOHNNIE: Do you really think so?

ANNE: Yes. In fact, she plays better than Tino. She wins more often than he does.

JOHNNIE: How can that be? Tino is stronger than Barbara, and he hits the ball harder.

ANNE: But he doesn't hit the ball as accurately as she does.

JOHNNIE: She probably gets more practice.

ANNE: You're right. Tino is busier than Barbara, so he can't play as often as she does.

JOHNNIE: Tino gets mad when he loses, doesn't he?

ANNE: Yes, he isn't a very good loser. Barbara accepts defeat more easily than Tino.

JOHNNIE: Why is that?

ANNE: Well, Tino takes tennis more seriously than most people. To Barbara it's just a game.

FREE RESPONSE • *Would you prefer to play tennis with Barbara or Tino? Why?*

COMPARISON OF ADVERBS

They don't play as well as we do.	They don't play as regularly as we do.
_____ poorly _____.	_____ seriously _____.
_____ hard _____.	_____ competitively _____.
_____ fast _____.	_____ energetically _____.

PRACTICE 1 • *Complete the sentences.*

Tino doesn't play as (good) as Barbara.   I don't walk as (slow) as you do.
Tino doesn't play as <u>well</u> as Barbara.   **I don't walk as <u>slowly</u> as you do.**

Our friends don't drive as (careful) as we do.
Our friends don't drive as <u>carefully</u> as we do.

1. Peter doesn't read as (quick) as Maria.
2. Gloria doesn't dance as (good) as Otis.
3. They don't dress as (fashionable) as we do.
4. Mrs. Bascomb doesn't speak as (loud) as her husband.
5. We don't live as (comfortable) as they do.
6. Jimmy doesn't study as (hard) as Linda.
7. Mr. Golo doesn't eat as (slow) as his wife.
8. They don't work as (careful) as we do.
9. You don't write as (poor) as Nick.

COMPARISON OF ADVERBS

We play better than they do.	We play more regularly than they do.
_____ worse _____.	_____ seriously _____.
_____ harder _____.	_____ competitively _____.
_____ faster _____.	_____ energetically _____.

PRACTICE 2 • *Complete the sentences.*

Barbara plays (good) than Tino.   He runs (fast) than she does.
Barbara plays <u>better</u> than Tino.   **He runs <u>faster</u> than she does.**

She hits the ball (accurate) than he does.
She hits the ball <u>more accurately</u> than he does.

1. Maria dresses (fashionable) than Nancy.
2. Mr. Bascomb works (hard) than his wife.
3. They live (expensive) than most people.
4. Anne sings (good) than I do.
5. Linda writes (careful) than Jimmy.
6. I speak (loud) than you do.
7. We work (fast) than our friends.
8. Jack drives (dangerous) than the average person.
9. Mr. and Mrs. Golo dance (bad) than we do.

Listen and repeat.

1. Tino could swim when he was nine years old.

2. Barbara could ski when she was sixteen years old.

3. Anne could play the guitar when she was twelve years old.

4. Otis could paint when he was seven years old.

5. Jimmy could play basketball when he was ten years old.

6. Nick could repair cars when he was seventeen years old.

PRACTICE • *Make a sentence for each picture in Nancy's photo album using* **could.**

one year old
Nancy could walk when she was one year old.

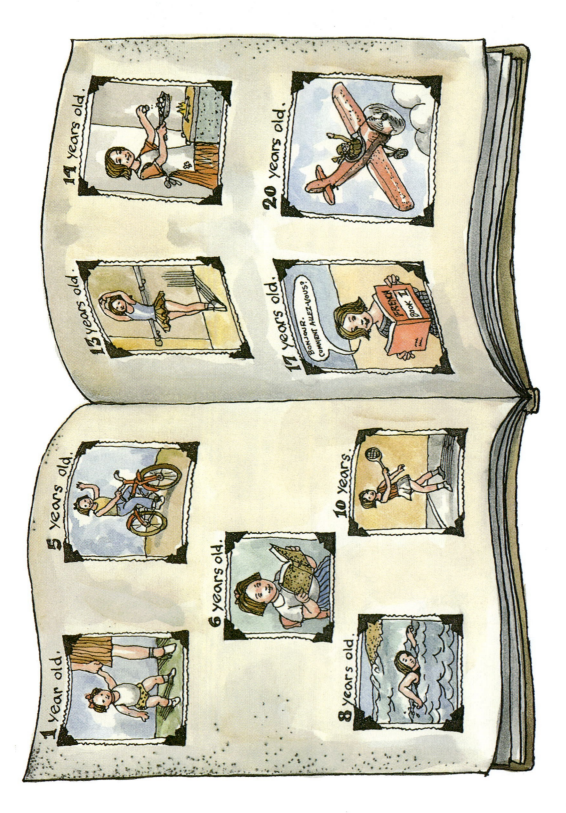

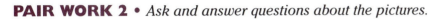

PAIR WORK I • *Ask and answer questions using* **could.**

A: **Could you swim when you were ten years old?**
B: **Yes, I could.** OR **No, I couldn't.**

1. ride a bicycle
2. play basketball
3. sail a boat
4. paint pictures
5. dance
6. play the piano
7. type
8. cook
9. repair a flat tire

PAIR WORK 2 • *Ask and answer questions about the pictures.*

1. A: **Did the police officer catch the robbers yesterday?**
   B: **No, he couldn't catch them because they were too fast.**

2. A: **Did Mrs. Golo feed the cat last night?**
   B: **No, she couldn't feed the cat because there wasn't any milk left.**

3. Did Suzi wash her hair this morning?

4. Did Johnnie move the piano yesterday?

5. Did Gloria visit the museum last weekend?

6. Did Barbara and Tino play tennis yesterday?

7. Did Linda finish her homework last night?

8. Did Marty go to the movies yesterday?

FREE RESPONSE • *Tell the class about something you couldn't do recently and explain why.*

Listen and practice.

PAIR WORK • *Have similar conversations.*

A: **I always do my homework.**	B: **So do I.**

1. A: I'm going to study tonight. B: _____.

2. A: I like to dance. B: _____.

3. A: I had a good time at the party. B: _____.

4. A: I can speak four languages. B: _____.

5. A: I'd like to visit Paris. B: _____.

6. A: I'll be busy tomorrow. B: _____.

7. A: I was very tired last night. B: _____.

8. A: I've worked hard this year. B: _____.

Listen and practice.

PAIR WORK • *Have similar conversations.*

A: **I'm not very hungry today.**   B: **Neither am I.**

1. A: I don't drink coffee anymore.   B: _____.

2. A: I can't play the piano.   B: _____.

3. A: I won't be here tomorrow.   B: _____.

4. A: I haven't seen Otis lately.   B: _____.

5. A: I wasn't home yesterday.   B: _____.

6. A: I didn't do my homework.   B: _____.

7. A: I couldn't go to the meeting.   B: _____.

8. A: I've never been to Mozambique.   B: _____.

Yesterday Jack went to Larry Sharp's New Car Lot to buy a new car. He drove there in his old car which he planned to use as a trade-in on the new one.

"Good afternoon," said Sharp, who smiled when he saw Jack. "It looks like you need a new car."

"I sure do," said Jack. "Could you show me one that will last as long as my old car, but won't give me as much trouble?"

Sharp pointed to a very large car. "Here's one that shouldn't give you any trouble. This car will drive much better than yours and will last twice as long."

"Yes, but my car could get thirty miles to the gallon when it was new. And I think mine still doesn't use as much gas as that one does."

"Well," said Sharp, "this one probably isn't as economical as yours, but it can go much faster than yours can."

Jack thought for a moment. "I really don't want a car that goes too fast. I probably drive more dangerously than most people do."

Then Sharp pointed to a much smaller car. "That car isn't as expensive as this big one. And it's as practical as your old car ever was. It will certainly drive better than yours."

Jack walked over to the small car and looked inside. "Could you start the engine for me?" he asked.

"Of course," said Sharp. "There. Do you like the sound of this engine as well as yours?" he smiled.

"There's no comparison. Mine sounds like a sick dog and this one sounds like a happy cat. I like it."

"But," interrupted Sharp, "this one will drive more slowly than even yours, while the *big* one . . ."

"Oh," said Jack, "I like the price of this one better than the big one. Here, let me sit in the driver's seat."

Sharp sat next to Jack and grinned. "But this car is too small for a man as big as you are. I really think you should get the big car."

Jack looked at Sharp. "No. I think I prefer this one. How much will you give me for my old car in trade for this one?"

"Well," said Sharp, thinking, "your car probably isn't as valuable as you think it is. It's certainly worth more to you than it is to me. I'll give you fifty dollars for it."

Jack turned off the engine of the little car and jumped out. "What!" he said. "Only fifty dollars for my old friend? A friend I've known as long as I've lived in this city? A friend that I know as well as I know myself? A friend that has been a true friend in sickness and in health?"

Jack went over to his old car, smiled at it, and got in. "No thank you, Mr. Sharp," said Jack. "Good-bye." He started up the loud old engine.

Sharp got out of the little car and just stood there, scratching his head. He watched Jack as he drove out of the lot and down the street as fast as he could go.

STORY QUESTIONS

1. Where did Jack go yesterday?
2. Why did he go there?
3. What are the advantages of the big car that Mr. Sharp wanted to sell Jack?
4. Why didn't Jack want a car that was too fast?
5. Did Jack like the small car that Mr. Sharp showed him?
6. How did he compare it to his own car?
7. Why did Mr. Sharp want to sell Jack the big car?
8. How much did Mr. Sharp offer to give Jack for his old car?
9. Why wasn't Jack happy with Mr. Sharp's offer?
10. What's your opinion of Larry Sharp?
11. Do you think he's a good salesman? Why or why not?
12. Would you like to buy a car from Larry Sharp?

READER'S THEATER • *Two students take the roles of Jack and Larry Sharp. A third student is the narrator. Read dramatically from the story.*

1. A: Do you think Gloria dances as well as Otis?
   B: **Yes, I do. I think she dances <u>better</u> than Otis.**

2. A: Do you think Anne sings as beautifully as Bonita Cantata?
   B: **No, I don't. I think Bonita Cantata sings <u>more beautifully</u> than Anne.**

3. Do you think Marty studies as hard as Jenny?

4. Do you think Miss Hackey lives as comfortably as Mr. Bascomb?

5. Do you think Tino runs as fast as Peter?

6. Do you think Stan works as carefully as Bruno?

7. Do you think Joe cooks as well as Mom?

8. Do you think Maria dresses as fashionably as Nancy?

PAIR WORK 1 • *Ask and answer the questions.*

> A: **Do you work as hard as the average person?**
> B: **Yes, I do. I work harder than the average person.**
>   OR   **No, I don't. The average person works harder than I do.**
>   OR   **About the same.**

1. Do you study as hard as the average student?
2. Do you talk faster than most people?
3. Do you dance better than your friends?
4. Does your father dress as well as your mother?
5. Does your mother sing as well as your father?

PAIR WORK 2 • *Make suggestions using "Why don't you . . . ?"*

> A: **I'm bored.**
> B: **Why don't you call your friends?**
>   OR   **Why don't you go to a movie?**

1. I'm thirsty.
2. I'm hungry.
3. I'm broke.
4. I'm lonely.
5. I'm tired.
6. It's cold in here.
7. The roof is leaking.
8. The windows are dirty.
9. There's no food in the refrigerator.
10. I need some stamps.

PAIR WORK 3 • *Have conversations using **so** and **neither**.*

> A: **I've had an interesting life.**   B: **So have I.**
>
> A: **I won't be here on Saturday.**   B: **Neither will I.**

1. A: I'm feeling good today.   B: _____.

2. A: I'm not tired at all.   B: _____.

3. A: I slept well last night.   B: _____.

4. A: I didn't watch TV yesterday.   B: _____.

5. A: I don't like most TV shows.   B: _____.

6. A: I want to travel more.   B: _____.

7. A: I'd like to visit Mozambique.   B: _____.

8. A: I've never been to Africa.   B: _____.

9. A: I can't fly an airplane.   B: _____.

10. A: I can ride a bicycle.   B: _____.

TALKING ABOUT PETS

1. Can you name the pets in the pictures?
2. Do you have a pet?
3. Do any of your neighbors have pets?
4. Why do so many people have dogs as pets?
5. What animal do you think is the most intelligent? playful?
6. What animal makes the best pet? Why?
7. What are the most popular pets in your country?
8. Do you think most pet owners treat their pets well?
9. Do you think some people treat their pets too well?

GROUP WORK • *Talk about your pets. If you don't own a pet, pretend you are the owner of one of the pets in the pictures above. Ask these questions and make up questions of your own.*

- What kind of pet do you have?
- What's your pet's name?
- What does your pet like to eat?
- Where does your pet sleep?

- Do you talk to your pet?
- Is your pet playful? intelligent? funny?
- Can your pet do tricks?
- Do you love your pet? Why?

COMPOSITION • *Write about your pet. What makes your pet special?*

GRAMMAR SUMMARY

COMPARISION OF ADJECTIVES AND ADVERBS

Maxie is	as	fast strong popular	as	the Champ.

He doesn't work	as	well hard carefully	as	I do.

I work	better harder more carefully	than	he does.

COULD Affirmative

I She They	could swim could speak French could read	when I was nine years old. as a child. before they went to school.

Negative

I He We	couldn't (could not)	go to the park have a picnic play tennis	yesterday because it was raining.

Interrogative

Could	you play the guitar? he ride a motorcycle last year? they sail a boat?

Short Answers

Yes,	I he they	could.	No,	I he they	couldn't.

SO

He is intelligent. They work hard. Anne can play the guitar. They've been to the museum. Maria went to the party. I'll pass the examination.	So	is she. do you. can Albert. have I. did Peter. will you.

NEITHER

Fred doesn't have a tie. They aren't very sophisticated. My sister can't swim. Jimmy hasn't eaten dinner. He didn't have any money. I won't take the bus.	Neither	does Barney. are you. can I. has Linda. did she. will you.

Review Chapter

8

TOPICS
Current issues
Jobs
Entertainment
Newspaper headlines
Your hometown

GRAMMAR
Review

FUNCTIONS
Giving opinions
Agreeing and disagreeing
Making excuses
Giving directions
Making complaints
Giving advice
Making recommendations

In the evening, young people in Wickam City often gather at the
Martinoli Restaurant. They eat, drink, tell stories, and have a good time.
Sometimes they talk about parties or make plans for the weekend, but
usually they just relax after a hard day of work.

One night last week, Otis and Gloria were sitting at a table with
Barbara and Tino. They were making plans for a picnic when Peter
came in with Maria Miranda. Peter and Maria seemed to be arguing
about something. They sat down with their friends and ordered a large
pizza. Maria was very excited. "Have you heard the news, Otis?" she
asked.

"No, what news?" said Otis.

"Banker Bascomb is running for mayor and
he plans to build a big toy factory in City Park."

"That's not news," said Tino. "Mr. Bascomb
runs for mayor every year, and he always
loses."

"Yes, but this year he doesn't have any
opposition. The present mayor is retiring, and
Mr. Bascomb is the only candidate. Besides,
there are a lot of people who think Wickam City
needs to grow. They want to see more industry
in this town, and they like the idea of a new toy
factory."

"OK. But they shouldn't build it in the middle
of City Park," said Otis. "The park is for people, not factories. Besides,
it's a great place to paint."

"Why does it have to be the park anyway?" said Barbara. "I mean, why don't they build the factory somewhere else, maybe on the edge of town?"

Peter replied, "Because the park is a very good location. You can get there easily from any part of the city. It has water and electricity, and there's plenty of room for expansion. Anyway, Mr. Bascomb has spoken to representatives of the toy company, and the only place they want to build their factory is in City Park."

"But Peter, it does seem sad," said Barbara. "What will happen to the little children who play there and the old people who sit on the park benches and feed the pigeons?"

"What about me?" said Tino. "Where will I play tennis? The private courts are too expensive."

"And me," said Maria. "Sometimes after a hard day at the hospital I'm very tired and nervous. Then I like to relax in the park and look at the flowers and trees. They're so beautiful. I hope nothing happens to the park."

"I know what you mean, Maria," said Peter softly. "After all, we met in the park. I like the park as much as anyone else, but as a businessman, I know that Wickam City needs more industry. A new factory will provide jobs and tax money for the city. We can use the money to improve our schools and build better roads. I call that progress. What do you think, Otis?"

"I'm sorry, Peter," he replied, "but I can't agree. I think there are things in life that people need more than money and progress. I think we need parks and flowers and trees to be happy. Even now, Wickam City has very little green space. It's difficult to hear a bird sing, and how can you put a price on a bird's song? I don't think it's progress to build a factory in City Park. It's a step backward."

"I'm going to run for mayor!"

"Why, Otis," said Gloria, "I've never seen you so serious."

"Well, Otis," said Peter, "if you really feel that way, what are you going to do about it?"

"I'm going to run for mayor," said Otis. "I'm going to oppose Mr. Bascomb and his ideas. My platform will be to save the park."

Everyone cheered and agreed that it was a wonderful idea. Even Peter was happy and ordered more lemonade for everyone.

"There's just one thing that bothers me," said Otis, scratching his head.

"What's that, Otis?"

"If I become mayor, I won't have any time to spend in the park."

STORY QUESTIONS

1. Where do young people in Wickam City often gather in the evening?
2. What do they do there?
3. Who was at the Martinoli Restaurant one night last week?
4. Why were Peter and Maria talking about Mr. Bascomb?
5. What does Mr. Bascomb plan to do?
6. Why doesn't Otis like the idea of a toy factory in City Park?
7. Why is the park a good location for a new factory?
8. What do little children and old people like to do in the park?
9. What does Tino like to do in the park?
10. What does Maria like to do there?
11. Why does Peter think it's progress to build a new factory in City Park?
12. Why doesn't Otis agree with Peter?
13. How is Otis going to save the park?
14. What is the one thing that worries Otis?

FREE RESPONSE

1. Do you think it's progress to build a new factory in City Park? Why or why not?
2. Do you think more business always means progress? Why or why not?
3. What is progress according to most people? What do you think?

GROUP WORK • *What are the most important issues people are talking about in your city? Is it the environment? the economy? education? jobs? taxes? crime? Discuss a current issue and give your opinions.*

Useful expressions:

What do you think about . . .	I don't know. It seems to me that . . .
I think we should . . .	We have to do something about . . .
That's a good point.	I disagree. I think . . .
Maybe you're right, but . . .	It isn't necessary because . . .
Don't you think . . .	That's not true.

 *Listen and practice.*

NICK: What's the matter, Fred? You look bored.

FRED: I *am* bored. I don't have anything to do.

NICK: Hmm, since you don't have anything to do, you can repair those tires for me.

FRED: Oh, I just remembered. I have to visit my sick aunt. See you later, Nick.

FREE RESPONSE • *Do you think Fred really has a sick aunt? What are some typical excuses people give when they don't want to do something?*

PAIR WORK • *Have conversations like the one above. Student A asks Student B to do a favor. Student B gives an excuse for not doing it. Try to use a different excuse in each situation.*

1. clean up . . .

2. wash . . .

3. mail . . .

4. take out . . .

5. sweep . . .

6. feed . . .

1. Tino Martinoli
   Waiter

2. Anne Jones
   Secretary

3. Richard Poole
   Teacher

4. Maria Miranda
   Doctor

5. Barney Field
   Taxi driver

6. Ula Hackey
   Actress

7. Susan Steel
   Police officer

8. Butch Hogan
   Professional wrestler

9. Lola Romantica
   Dance teacher

FREE RESPONSE • *Answer the questions about jobs.*

1. How much do you think these people make (per day, per hour, etc.)?
2. Do you think everyone should get the same pay?
3. What are their duties?
4. What are the qualifications for these jobs? For example, to be a waiter you should have a good memory and a friendly personality.
5. Talk about the advantages and disadvantages of the different jobs. For example, a waiter gets free meals and sometimes meets interesting people in the restaurant. On the other hand, he has to be on his feet all the time.
6. Which job is the most interesting? dangerous? exciting? boring? difficult?
7. Which job is the easiest? best? worst?
8. Which job would you like to have? Why?

WRITTEN EXERCISE • *Complete the sentences with an appropriate adjective or adverb.*

Jack laughs (easy) _more easily_ than Fred.

I don't type as (slow) _slowly_ as my brother.

Wickam City is (noisy) _noisier_ than Colterville.

Colterville is the (peaceful) _most peaceful_ town I've ever seen.

1. Mrs. Golo drives (bad) _____ than her husband.

2. She's the (bad) _____ driver I've ever seen.

3. Sam gives his time (generous) _____ than most people.

4. He's one of the (respected) _____ men in town.

5. My dog is (big) _____ and (smart) _____ than yours.

6. Barbara doesn't get mad as (easy) _____ as Tino.

7. She's a (good) _____ loser than he is.

8. Jimmy doesn't write as (carefully) _____ as his sister.

9. She studies (hard) _____ than the average person.

10. Mr. Bascomb is (practical) _____ than his wife.

11. She's (friendly) _____ than he is.

12. We don't understand business as (good) _____ as they do.

PRACTICE • *Combine the sentences using **who**.*

A girl entered the shop. She was wearing a red dress.
The girl who entered the shop was wearing a red dress.

Some people visited Dr. Pasto. They were from New York.
The people who visited Dr. Pasto were from New York.

1. A man called the office. He wanted some information.
2. A woman owns the company. She's very rich.
3. A boy found my watch. He lives across the street.
4. Some children were playing in the park. They seemed to be very happy.
5. A girl painted that picture. She's a good artist.
6. A man repaired my television. He did a good job.
7. A woman gave the party. She's a friend of mine.
8. Some people arrived late. They had the wrong address.
9. A girl sang at the party. She had a terrible voice.
10. A man prepared the food. He was a bad cook.
11. Some people left early. They weren't having a good time.
12. A woman asked me for my phone number. She was six feet tall.

WICKAM DAILY NEWS

Fire Leaves 30 People Homeless

Up to thirty people were left homeless by a fire that badly damaged the Royal Apartments. "This is a tragedy," Fire Captain Jack Winters said. "Everything these people have is in those four walls."

More than forty firefighters battled the blaze that began about 9:30 A.M., bringing it under control in an hour. Three occupants were hurt in the blaze, including one person who injured his leg jumping from a window. The cause of the blaze is unknown.

Jackson Enters Race for Mayor

Otis Jackson has announced that he will be a candidate for mayor of Wickam City. He will run against John Bascomb, president of City Bank. Mr. Jackson promises to protect the environment if he becomes mayor. He criticized Mr. Bascomb's plan to build a toy factory in City Park.

"We have only one park," said Mr. Jackson. "We must save it. Parks are for people, not factories. That's why I'm running for mayor—I want to save City Park for the people."

GROUP WORK 1 • *Talk about some interesting events in the news this week. Ask information questions with **who, what, when, where,** and **why.***

GROUP WORK 2 • *Choose one of these headlines and make up an interesting story about it. One student starts the story, another student tells what happens next, and so on.*

80-year-old Man Marries Teenager	**Homeless Woman Wins $5 Million**	**Boy Teaches Dog to Speak**	**New Pill Makes You Smarter**

CLASS ACTIVITY • *Groups take turns telling their stories. Other students ask questions.*

WRITTEN EXERCISE • *Complete the sentences.*

The woman I spoke to *gave me some good information.*
was very intelligent.

1. The man she loves _____

2. The company he works for _____

3. The city we live in _____

4. The person you told me about _____

5. The woman I met at the party _____

6. The clothes she wears _____

7. The boy Linda danced with _____

8. The restaurant you recommended _____

9. The people we live next to _____

10. The girl I talked to _____

FREE RESPONSE 1 • *Do you agree with these opinions? If not, change them so that they are true for you.*

1. French is the most beautiful language in the world.
2. New York is the most exciting city in the world.
3. The evening news is the most interesting program on TV.
4. Teachers are the most important members of society.
5. Germans are the most industrious people in the world.
6. Luciano Pavarotti is the greatest singer of our time.
7. Italian cooking is the best in the world.
8. Brazilian women are the most beautiful in the world.
9. The automobile is the greatest invention of all time.
10. The most enjoyable way to travel is by ship.

FREE RESPONSE 2 • *Answer the questions using phrasal verbs.*

1. Are you putting aside (saving) your money to buy something special?
2. When was the last time you gave away something?
3. Do you always try on clothes before you buy them?
4. How often do you turn up late for meetings?
5. When was the last time you put off something?
6. When you have an important decision to make, do you always think it over carefully?
7. Have you ever turned down an interesting offer?
8. Have you taken up any new hobbies this year?
9. Are you looking forward to anything special this month?
10. When was the last time you dressed up for a special occasion?

• *Look at the map and take notes as you listen to Mr. Bascomb give the Farleys directions to his house.*

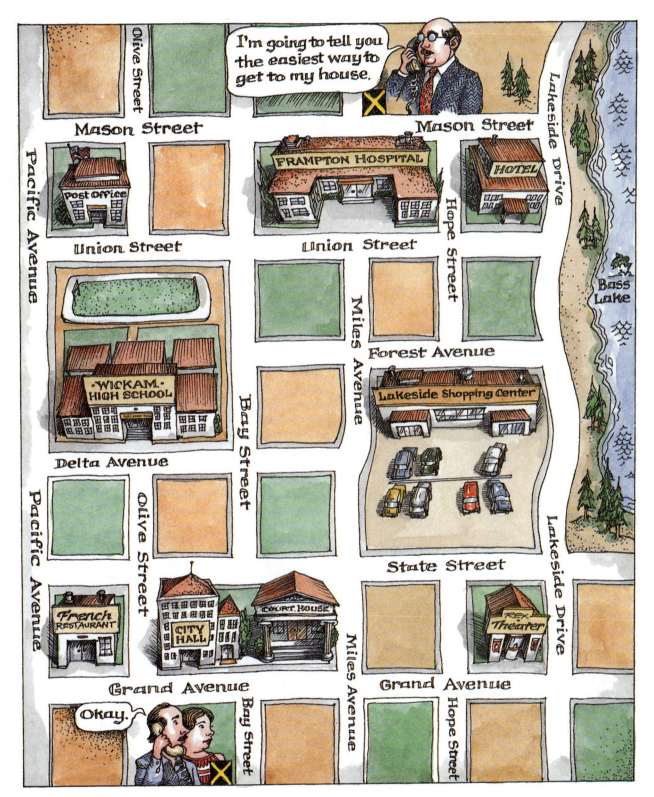

GROUP WORK • *Mr. Bascomb told Mr. Farley the easiest way to get to his house, but it's not the fastest way. Look at the map and figure out the fastest way to Mr. Bascomb's house. Write the directions on a separate piece of paper.*

WRITTEN EXERCISE • *Complete the sentences about the people in the pictures using these adjectives:* **tired, happy, sick, embarrassed, bored, afraid, surprised, sad, angry.**

1. Peter *is embarrassed*.

2. Mrs. Golo _____

3. Albert _____

4. Linda _____

5. Tino _____

6. Gina _____

7. Sam _____

8. Anne _____

9. Fred _____

PAIR WORK • *Ask and answer questions about the pictures.*

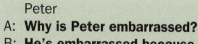

Peter
A: **Why is Peter embarrassed?**
B: **He's embarrassed because he doesn't have any money.**

FREE RESPONSE

1. When was the last time you were in an embarrassing situation? What happened?
2. When was the last time you were surprised? What happened?
3. When was the last time you didn't feel well? What was the matter? What did you do about it? How long did it take you to get well?
4. What scares you? Are you afraid of the dark? heights? crowded elevators?
5. What makes you happy? Do you think it's possible to be happy all the time?
6. What makes you sad? What do you do when you're feeling sad?
7. Do you work or study too hard? Are you tired today? When was the last time you had a day off?
8. When was the last time you were angry about something? What happened?
9. Are you ever bored? What do you do in your free time?

COMPOSITION • *Write a short paragraph about a time when you were very surprised, happy, sad, angry, or afraid. What were the circumstances?*

WRITTEN EXERCISE • *Rewrite the sentences using the adverbs indicated.*

(yet) Anne isn't here. *Anne isn't here yet.*

(still) We're waiting for her. *We're still waiting for her.*

(perhaps) She's working late. *Perhaps she's working late.*

1. (really) Maria likes her job. _____
2. (much) She works harder than most people. _____
3. (recently) We haven't seen Peter. _____
4. (maybe) He's out of town. _____
5. (very) Barbara is worried. _____
6. (anywhere) She can't find her keys. _____
7. (just) Jack has left his apartment. _____
8. (probably) He's gone to the park. _____
9. (again) I'd like to talk with you. _____
10. (here) Let's meet tomorrow. _____
11. (yet) We haven't been to the beach. _____
12. (unfortunately) The weather has been bad. _____
13. (still) Is Sandy working at the office? _____
14. (soon) I hope she'll come home. _____

PRACTICE • *Answer the questions about today's entertainment in Wickam City. Look at the entertainment guide on page 138.*

1. Where is *Dream Lover* playing?
2. Who's the star of the movie?
3. Is it a comedy or a love story?
4. What time is the last show?
5. What kind of music do the Beach Bums play?
6. Where are they performing tonight?
7. What time is their first show?
8. How much are the best seats?
9. What time is the boxing match?
10. Who is "Choo Choo" Kelly going to fight tonight?
11. How much are the cheapest seats?
12. Where's the place to go if you don't have any money?

CONVERSATION

Listen and repeat.

GROUP WORK • *You and your friends are trying to decide what to do tonight. Look at the entertainment guide and discuss the different possibilities. Decide (a) where to go, (b) what time you're going to go, and (c) how you're going to get there.*

CLASS ACTIVITY • *Mr. Bascomb is having dinner at the Magnolia Restaurant. It's his first time at the restaurant and he doesn't like it. Look at the picture and tell what's wrong.*

ROLE PLAY • *Mr. Bascomb calls the manager to complain about the restaurant. The manager thinks there's nothing wrong. What do they say to each other? Act out the conversation between Mr. Bascomb and the manager.*

MR. BASCOMB: This soup is terrible!

MANAGER: What are you talking about? There's nothing wrong with the soup . . .

COMPOSITION • *The next day, Mr. Bascomb writes a letter complaining to the owner of the Magnolia Restaurant, a man named Horace Grabski. Complete Mr. Bascomb's letter.*

Dear Mr. Grabski:

    Last night I had dinner at the Magnolia Restaurant, and it was the worst experience of my life. First of all, the food was . . .

Got a problem?

Ask Sophie

Dear Sophie,

My husband and I are having a dinner party at our home next week. All of our dearest friends will be there. Unfortunately, my husband wants to invite his brother to the party. His brother has terrible manners, and I'm afraid he'll ruin the party. What should I do?

Concerned

Dear Concerned,

You should invite your brother-in-law to the party. After all, he's a member of your family. But your husband should talk to him about the importance of good manners.

GROUP WORK 1 • *Read the following letters to Sophie. What do you think these people should do about their problems?*

1. Dear Sophie,

   I've just moved to Chicago from a small town in Texas. I don't know anyone here, and I'm very lonely. How can I meet people and make friends?

   Lonely in Chicago

2. Dear Sophie,

   My wife and I get invitations to a lot of social events. We're always late because she takes so long to get ready. Sometimes I have to wait an hour while she puts on her makeup. I think it's important to be on time, but my wife is more concerned about her looks. What do you think?

   Henry

3. Dear Sophie,

   Every time I go to the market or the post office, someone comes up and asks me for money. I know many of these people really need help. But some of them are just lazy. I can't give money to everyone who asks for it. What should I do?

   Confused

4. Dear Sophie,

   There's a very cute guy who just moved into my apartment building. I would love to meet him. How can I break the ice?

   Jane

5. Dear Sophie,

   My mother-in-law, who lives in another state, is coming here next month. My wife wants her mother to stay with us while she's in town, but I say no. Her mother is a pain in the neck. The last time she was here, she made my life miserable. What do you suggest?

   Richard

6. Dear Sophie,

   Last month I went to a very elegant party, and I met the girl of my dreams. I've called her several times, and we've had some wonderful conversations, but I'm afraid to ask her for a date. I have very little money, and I drive an old beat-up car. How can I impress this special person?

   Bill

GROUP WORK 2 • *Write a letter to Sophie about a problem you're having. Read your letter to other students and get their advice.*

FREE RESPONSE

1. What were you doing yesterday morning at ten o'clock?
2. Where did you go last Sunday? What did you do?
3. How much exercise do you get? Do you like to take long walks?
4. Do you plan to take up a new hobby or sport this year?
5. What are some things you like to do? Hate to do?
6. What are you going to do this weekend?
7. Where will you spend your next vacation?
8. Have you made any important decisions recently?
9. What is your greatest ambition?

PRACTICE • *Add tag questions to the sentences.*

Gloria is out of town.	You haven't seen her.
Gloria is out of town, isn't she?	**You haven't seen her, have you?**

1. Barbara has gone to the park.
2. She didn't take the bus.
3. She got a ride with Tino.
4. They're going to have a picnic.
5. They aren't going to play tennis.
6. Maria will be there.
7. She likes picnics.
8. Peter can't go to the picnic.
9. He has to work.
10. He doesn't have much free time.
11. It's supposed to be sunny today.
12. You don't think it will rain.

WRITTEN EXERCISE • *Complete the sentences using the present perfect or the past simple.*

Mr. Bascomb (work) ___*has worked*___ at the City Bank for twenty years.

He (become) ___*became*___ president five years ago.

1. Maria (see) _____ that movie three times.

2. She (see) _____ it again yesterday.

3. Dr. Pasto (have) _____ a very interesting life.

4. He (visit) _____ China when he (be) _____ a young man.

5. He (write) _____ several books about his travels in the past ten years.

6. Sam and Jack (be) _____ friends for a long time.

7. They (know) _____ each other since high school.

8. Jack (go) _____ to the park every day last week.

9. He (go) _____ to the park only once this week.

10. Gloria (take) _____ her car to the garage yesterday.

11. She (have) _____ a lot of trouble with it recently.

12. I (speak) _____ to her on the phone a little while ago.

ROLE PLAY 1

Student A plays Peter, Student B plays Sandy, and Student C plays the waiter.
Situation: Peter and Sandy have just finished their lunch and the waiter is showing Peter the bill. Peter is very embarrassed because he doesn't have any money. He asks the waiter if he can pay next week. The waiter says no. Sandy offers to help.

ROLE PLAY 2

You meet someone at a party who is going to visit your hometown or your favorite city for the first time. He or she asks you for information. Have a conversation like the one above and include these questions:

- When is the best time to visit?
- What's the weather like then?
- Can you recommend a good hotel?
- What places do you think I should see?

- What are the people like?
- What's the food like?
- Are there good places to go shopping?
- Where should I go for a good time?

COMPOSITION • Write about a city you would like to visit. Why would you like to go there? What's it like?

1. She only has _____ free time on the weekends.

   a. much   c. a little
   b. a few   d. any

2. He doesn't drink _____ coffee.

   a. much   c. a little
   b. some   d. many

3. They don't know _____ people in Florida.

   a. much   c. a few
   b. some   d. many

4. There are _____ magazines in the living room.

   a. any   c. much
   b. a few   d. a little

5. We bought _____ food today.

   a. much   c. a lot of
   b. many   d. plenty

6. None of those glasses are clean.

   _____ of them are dirty.

   a. Some   c. Both
   b. All   d. Many

7. I don't think there's _____ home.

   a. any person   c. any people
   b. someone   d. anyone

8. She has _____ in her handbag.

   a. something   c. a thing
   b. some thing   d. anything

9. He was late _____ he took a taxi.

   a. as   c. then
   b. so   d. since

10. Unfortunately, I _____ wash the dishes now.

    a. can   c. have to
    b. like to   d. try to

11. I think that man is a burglar.

    _____ I call the police?

    a. Could   c. Shall
    b. Will   d. Would

12. _____ you open the window, please?

    a. Could   c. Should
    b. Shall   d. Must

13. Mr. Bascomb works very hard. He _____ relax more.

    a. likes to   c. shall
    b. would   d. should

14. Barbara _____ like to play tennis tomorrow.

    a. shall   c. can
    b. would   d. will

15. She _____ play tennis yesterday because it was raining.

    a. won't   c. couldn't
    b. can't   d. shouldn't

16. Barney is very happy. He _____ like his job.

    a. should   c. must
    b. will   d. has to

17. Mrs. Golo is fond of her students. She's giving _____ some candy.

    a. them   c. they
    b. to them   d. for them

18. My sister called last week. I haven't spoken _____ since.

    a. him   c. her
    b. she   d. to her

19. Peter received a letter _____ France yesterday.

    a. to   c. of
    b. by   d. from

20. He has an apartment _____ Maple Street.
    a. at
    b. on
    c. in
    d. between

21. The girls are washing _____ clothes.
    a. there
    b. theirs
    c. their
    d. them

22. _____ some paper on the desk.
    a. It has
    b. They're
    c. There are
    d. There's

23. Jimmy isn't _____ to vote.
    a. very old
    b. enough old
    c. old enough
    d. old for

24. People respect Dr. Pasto. They _____ him because of his great knowledge.
    a. look up to
    b. look at
    c. look up
    d. look for

25. Sandy likes the green dress. She's _____ now.
    a. trying for it
    b. trying them on
    c. trying it on
    d. trying on it

26. Have you been to the post office? Yes, I _____.
    a. did
    b. have
    c. go
    d. was

27. You don't like hamburgers, _____?
    a. you don't
    b. you do
    c. don't you
    d. do you

28. That's the _____ dog I've ever seen.
    a. smarter
    b. smartest
    c. more smart
    d. most smart

29. The living room is _____ than the kitchen.
    a. bigger
    b. more bigger
    c. biggest
    d. more big

30. They work in the _____ building in Wickam City.
    a. modern
    b. modernest
    c. more modern
    d. most modern

31. She dances as _____ as he does.
    a. good
    b. better
    c. well
    d. fine

32. They live _____ than we do.
    a. comfortable
    b. comfortably
    c. more comfortably
    d. much comfortably

33. She runs _____ than her brother.
    a. faster
    b. as fast
    c. fastest
    d. more fast

34. I have _____ experience than you do.
    a. as much
    b. less
    c. a little
    d. fewer

35. They _____ the dishes when she left.
    a. was washing
    b. were washing
    c. are washing
    d. have washed

36. At eight o'clock last night I _____ a book.
    a. was reading
    b. read
    c. have read
    d. am reading

37. He was working at the office when the telegram _____.
    a. was arriving
    b. arrived
    c. has arrived
    d. arrives

38. Our friends _____ in town since last Monday and they are still here.
    a. are
    b. were
    c. will be
    d. have been

39. They _____ to the park yet.
    a. didn't go
    b. have gone
    c. haven't gone
    d. don't go

40. We _____ a good movie last week.
    a. saw   c. were seeing
    b. have seen   d. see

41. Has Linda finished her homework yet?

    Yes, she _____ it a little while ago.

    a. finishes   c. has finished
    b. finished   d. is finished

42. This is the first time I _____ tennis this month.

    a. play   c. have played
    b. am playing   d. played

43. Albert has gone to the market _____ some eggs.

    a. for buying   c. for buy
    b. to buy   d. buy

44. Sam likes to _____ on the weekends.

    a. go fish   c. go fishing
    b. go to fish   d. do fishing

45. He _____ play basketball in high school.

    a. use to   c. like to
    b. used to   d. always

46. I didn't _____ like Chinese food.

    a. use to   c. used
    b. used to   d. usually

47. They don't have _____ to go.

    a. nowhere   c. any where
    b. somewhere   d. anywhere

48. She has a meeting _____.

    a. to go   c. to attend
    b. to see   d. to visit

49. We took the oranges _____ were in the refrigerator.

    a. that   c. there
    b. who   d. those

50. Do you know the man _____ lives across the street?

    a. which   c. who
    b. there   d. what

Preview

Teacher, see page x.

GRAMMAR
Present perfect continuous
Might
First conditional
Second conditional

We use the **present perfect continuous** for an action that began in the past and is still continuing or has only just finished.

Otis and Gloria have been picking flowers.

Sandy has been cleaning her apartment.

PAIR WORK • *Ask and answer questions using the **present perfect continuous**.*

> 1. A: **What have Luisa and Carlos been doing?**
>   B: **They've been eating dinner.**

1. Luisa and Carlos

2. Anne

3. the boys

4. Fred

5. Elmer and Sarah

6. Suzi

7. Jimmy

8. Linda and Bob

9. Nick

We use **might** to talk about possible actions in the future.

WRITTEN EXERCISE • *Add sentences using* **might.**

If the action in the if-clause happens, it is quite possible that the action in the result clause will happen. If Linda stays in the sun too long, she'll get a sunburn.

NOTE: The verb in the if-clause is in the present tense. The verb in the main clause is in the future tense.

WRITTEN EXERCISE • *Complete these conditional sentences.*

If Mrs. Golo had more free time, she would take dancing lessons. But in truth, she has very little free time, so she won't take dancing lessons.

If Bob were President of the United States, he would give a big party at the White House. But he isn't President of the United States, so he won't give a party at the White House.

NOTE: In the second conditional, the verb in the if-clause is in the past tense; the verb in the result clause is in the conditional tense: **would** + base form of verb.

PAIR WORK • *Ask and answer questions about these situations.*

1. What would you do if you had a million dollars?

2. What would you do if a homeless person asked you for money?

3. What would you do if you found a burglar in your home?

4. What would you do if you were a guest for dinner at your friend's house and you didn't like the food?

5. What would you do if you saw your neighbor's house on fire?

6. What would you do if you had only six months to live?

Appendix

INFINITIVE	PAST TENSE	PAST PARTICIPLE	INFINITIVE	PAST TENSE	PAST PARTICIPLE
be	was	been	lay	laid	laid
become	became	become	lead	led	led
bet	bet	bet	leave	left	left
break	broke	broken	lose	lost	lost
bring	brought	brought	make	made	made
build	built	built	meet	met	met
buy	bought	bought	put	put	put
catch	caught	caught	read	read	read
come	came	come	ride	rode	ridden
cut	cut	cut	run	ran	run
do	did	done	see	saw	seen
drink	drank	drunk	sell	sold	sold
drive	drove	driven	shine	shone	shone
eat	ate	eaten	sing	sang	sung
feed	fed	fed	sit	sat	sat
feel	felt	felt	sleep	slept	slept
fight	fought	fought	speak	spoke	spoken
find	found	found	spend	spent	spent
fly	flew	flown	stand	stood	stood
forget	forgot	forgotten	steal	stole	stolen
get	got	got	swim	swam	swum
give	gave	given	take	took	taken
go	went	gone	teach	taught	taught
grow	grew	grown	tell	told	told
have	had	had	think	thought	thought
hear	heard	heard	understand	understood	understood
hide	hid	hidden	wake	woke	waked
hit	hit	hit	wear	wore	worn
hold	held	held	win	won	won
know	knew	known	write	wrote	written

MR. BASCOMB: I'm going to tell you the easiest way to get to my house.

MR. FARLEY: OK.

MR. BASCOMB: Go to Grand Avenue and turn right. Then go down three blocks to Lakeside Drive.

MR. FARLEY: Three blocks to Lakeside. OK.

MR. BASCOMB: Turn left on Lakeside and go up four blocks until you come to Mason Street.

MR. FARLEY: OK.

MR. BASCOMB: Go left onto Mason. Then, after two blocks, look for the yellow house on the corner, across from Frampton Hospital.

MR. FARLEY: The yellow house on the corner?

MR. BASCOMB: That's it.

MR. FARLEY: OK. We're leaving now.

MR. BASCOMB: See you soon.

MR. FARLEY: Good-bye.

ask out = invite someone to do something (go to a show, a meal)
He asked her out to a movie.

be against = oppose
I'm against building a toy factory in City Park.

be back = return
I'm going to the drugstore. I'll be back in fifteen minutes.

be fed up with = be completely bored
I'm fed up with working. I want to have some fun.

be over = be finished
The meeting will be over in a few minutes.

break into = enter illegally, especially by force (a bank, a building, a house, etc.)
Last month a burglar broke into my apartment and took the TV.

bring up = mention or introduce a subject
You can bring up the question of child care at the next meeting.

call off = cancel (an event, an arrangement, an activity)
We had to call off the picnic because of rain.

catch up with = reach (someone who is ahead)
He was walking fast. I had to run to catch up with him.

cheer up = become happier
My sister was feeling depressed, but she cheered up when you invited her to the party.

come up with = think of, produce (an idea, a plan, a suggestion)
We must come up with a plan to improve the economy.

count on = depend on, rely on (someone)
If you ever need help, you can always count on me.

do without = manage in the absence of a person or thing
I like coffee, but I can do without it.

feel up to = feel strong enough (to do something)
I'm very tired. I don't feel up to playing tennis.

figure out = understand (someone or something) with difficulty
I can't figure out why she married Bill. He has nothing to offer.

fill in = complete (a form, a questionnaire)
It took me fifteen minutes to fill in the application form.

find out = discover after making an effort
How did you find out that she was living in Paris?

get away = escape; be free to leave
The police chased the bandit, but he got away.

get away with = do something wrong or illegal without being punished
She always cheats on her exams. I don't know how she gets away with it.

get back = reach home again
We spent the whole day at the beach and didn't get back until after dark.

get over = recover from (an illness, a shock, a disappointment)
I had the flu last week, but I got over it quickly.

get through = finish, complete (some work, a job, a book)
She had a lot of work to do yesterday, but she got through all of it.

give in = stop resisting; surrender
Her boyfriend didn't want to go dancing, but he finally gave in.

give up = stop trying to do something (often because it is too difficult)
He tried to pick some oranges, but he couldn't reach them so he gave up.

go ahead = proceed; continue
Go ahead. Don't wait for me.

go away = leave; leave this place
Go away! I don't want to see you!

go on = continue any action
Go on with your story. It's very interesting.

go out = go to a social event (as to go to a theater, concert)
She has a lot of friends and goes out a lot.

grow up = become adult
Children grow up very fast nowadays.

hold on = wait (especially on the telephone)
"Hold on. I'll be with you in a minute."

hold up = rob
Two gunmen held up the National Bank last week.

leave out = omit
When he filled out the application form, he left out his phone number.

let down = disappoint someone (often by breaking a promise or agreement)
You let me down. You promised to help me, but you didn't.

look after = take care of (someone or something)
My neighbor looks after the dog while I'm away.

look forward to = expect with pleasure
We're looking forward to the party next week.

look up = visit someone
She looked up her uncle when she was in San Francisco.

look up to = respect; admire
People look up to Dr. Pasto because of his great knowledge.

make up for = compensate for (a mistake, doing or not doing something)
I'm sorry I forgot your birthday, but I'll make it up to you.

move out = leave a house or apartment with one's possessions
Our neighbors moved out of their apartment yesterday.

pick up = get, collect (something or someone)
She picked up a package at the post office.

pick up = give someone a ride in a vehicle
He picked up his girlfriend after work and drove her home.

point out = show; explain
She pointed out that a small car is more practical than a big car.

put back = return; replace (something)
When you finish looking at the magazines, put them back on the shelf.

put off = delay or postpone (doing something until a later time)
Never put off until tomorrow what you can do today.

put up with = suffer; tolerate (a difficult situation or person)
Our neighbors make a lot of noise, and we have to put up with it.

run into = meet someone by chance
I was on my way home when I ran into an old friend.

run out of = use all of and have none left (money, time, patience)
She ran out of money and had to borrow some from me.

see about = make inquiries or arrangements
We called the travel agency to see about getting a flight to New York.

see off = say good-bye to someone who is going on a trip
I saw my brother off at the airport last Sunday.

stand up for = defend verbally
Her mother criticized her, but her father stood up for her.

take off = remove an article of clothing
It was very hot, so he took off his coat.

take over = become the person or group in charge
He took over the business after his father died.

take up = begin a hobby, sport, or kind of study
Last year she took up stamp collecting, and now it's her favorite pastime.

talk over = discuss a matter with someone else
Whenever he has a problem, he talks it over with his wife.

think over = consider carefully (a problem, an offer, a situation)
You don't have to make a decision right away. Go home and think it over.

try on = put on (an article of clothing) to see how it fits
She tried on several dresses before finding one she liked.

try out = test
You should try out the typewriter before buying it.

turn down = refuse, reject (an offer, an application, an applicant)
He applied for a job at the bank but was turned down.

turn out = result, develop, or end
Don't worry. Everything will turn out all right.

turn up/down = increase/decrease (volume, force, pressure)
Would you please turn down the radio? It's too loud.

wear out = use (something) until it is finished
He has worn out three pairs of shoes in the last year.

work out = find the solution to a problem
We don't have enough money to pay all our expenses, but we'll work things out somehow.

PRONUNCIATION

CHAPTER ONE

m	n		ng		
come	ten	dinner	long	bring	singer
home	pen	winner	song	young	singing
same	thin	thinner	ring	wedding	ringing
time	begin	beginner	thing	building	bringing

The game will begin at ten past nine.
The thin swimmer is the winner.
Take him some ham for dinner.

The young couple is buying a wedding ring.
He's bringing his painting this evening.
She's making something interesting.

Slim is buying a young chicken for dinner.
The phone is ringing in the living room.
Sam sang the same song nine times.

CHAPTER TWO

l			r		
like	dollar	family	rest	order	work
look	belong	hotel	radio	corner	care
love	college	small	ripe	camera	her
leave	help	pull	repeat	very	your

The tall policeman seldom smiled.
He left a small yellow envelope by the telephone.
Sally lived alone in a small hotel.

He drove a red truck to work every day.
Where was your sister yesterday morning?
We never drink water in the afternoon.

The yellow roses are lovely.
Your girlfriend always arrives late to work.
She wrote a long letter to her brother last Friday.

CHAPTER THREE

v			f			
vase	driver	serve	for	often	leaf	enough
very	travel	have	fun	defend	half	philosophy
visit	evening	leave	fast	laughing	safe	
never	movie	save	free	telephone	life	

She gave me a very expensive vase.
We've never visited the University.

The friendly philosopher often laughs at his wife.
She found a knife and fork on the shelf.

My friend never leaves the office before half past five.
He often drives very fast.

CHAPTER FIVE

æ

ask	bad	factory
after	plan	fantastic
animal	fast	telegram
address	dance	mechanic

The fat man handed a telegram to the bandit.
The happy dancer had a fantastic plan.

ə

ugly	some	country
under	club	discuss
oven	young	recover
lunch	study	Monday

The summer months are lovely in the country.
Someone is coming from the truck.

Jack had some unhappy customers last Sunday.
Is someone standing in front of the bank?

CHAPTER SIX

dž

job	pigeon	large
just	engine	message
journey	original	strange
generous	pajamas	knowledge

The average vegetarian likes orange juice.
I've just eaten a strange Japanese vegetable.
The energetic stranger began his dangerous journey.

tš

chair	teacher	lunch
cheap	statue	peach
chase	lecture	which
church	situation	catch

She had lunch with the charming French teacher.
He reached for the peach that was on the chair.
Which statue is the cheapest?

The large peaches and oranges are in the kitchen.
Did they change the subject of the lecture?
I don't have much knowledge of the Japanese culture.

CHAPTER SEVEN

u

good	would	put
book	could	cookie
look	should	neighborhood

I couldn't get a good look at the cook.
The good-looking football player took my cookies.

uw

who	soup	stupid
shoe	mood	student
true	noon	shampoo
food	lose	pollution

Did Mr. Poole lose his spoon yesterday afternoon?
Whose shampoo is in the living room?

The stupid cook put sugar in my soup.
Those students should be in a good mood.

VOCABULARY

CHAPTER ONE

adventurous
age (n.)
artistic
athletic
attractive
average (adj.)

barn
bellboy
break (v.)

choice
coin
coworker
cure (v.)

decision

economical
elegant
exercise (n.)
explain

farmhouse
fast (adj.)
fly away
foot

gallon
gate

hand (n.)

healthy
hurt

inch
industrious

light (adj.)
low

maid
maximum
mileage
million
mood

nothing

offer (v.)

paycheck
population
powerful
practical

raise (n.)
remedy

salary
severely
solid
speed (n.)
stingy

stream
successful

toilet paper
twice

volunteer

weigh
winner

Expressions

It's a long way from town.
It's later than you think.

He was in a bad mood.
They're good at their jobs.

Can I have a raise?
I can't live on this salary.

Get out of here!
Get back to work!

Trust me.
I give up.

How about a date, baby?
That's impossible!

CHAPTER TWO

application
apply

become
burn (v.)

change (v.)
childhood
commission
crop (n.)

destroy

economics
engaged
engagement

farmer

glasses
grow

high school
hopeless

insect

lay (v.)
lifeguard

marriage
minimum

necessary

qualifications

raise (v.)
recently
relationship
ring (n.)

serious
similar
since (adv.)
since (conj.)
since (prep.)
slice (v.)
suffer

tour manager

yardwork

Expressions

Is it still open?
Where are you located?

The story took place in Paris.
Sounds interesting.

That's no good.
It's hopeless.

Didn't you know?
At least . . .

similar interests
local references

full time
part time

CHAPTER THREE

adventure   exotic   makeup   receive   yet
alive   motion   reputation   yourself
ambition   forest   mountain   ridiculous
             fresh   river
cage   next (adv.)
calmly   horseback riding   seafood
camping   parrot   second (n.)
cookbook   live (adj.)   pick up   ship
                             pirate   specialty
deep   mail (n.)
deliver   mail carrier   raw   travel agency

Expressions

How's everything?   This place is really something.   I got tired of it.
What's happened?   This place is for the birds.   I can hardly wait.

Tell me about yourself.   It's supposed to be out of this world.   Right now.
Are you serious?   They have some friends in common.   a flat tire

CHAPTER FOUR

article   handkerchief   master   sadly
                  hero   selection
baggy   Honda   newsstand   shake
big band music   huge   nowadays   shoulder
bike   snow-white
brag (v.)   jump off   observe   someday
               jump on
fewer   rack   terrific
               kid   ride (n.)   throw
gold   king   roar (n.)   tramp
gray-haired   roar (v.)   trust
guess (v.)   line
               lottery   wrinkle

Expressions

Make sure he gets it.   Darn it!   That's life.
I'll be happy to.   What's so great about him?   Times change.

We danced cheek-to-cheek.   He doesn't mind as long as   I'd better go.
Nobody thinks anything of it.   you put the magazines back.   So long, kid.

Congratulations!   Who's responsible for this?
That's what counts.   It's his fault.

CHAPTER FIVE

affect (v.)
ambitious
anthropology

bravery
bright

captain
coach
competitive
complaint
compliment

danger
doubt (n.)

edition
end (n.)
enjoyable
even

face (v.)
feature (adj.)

generosity

government
groom (n.)

head (n.)
himself

impress
impressive
intelligence

kindness

lake
league
loyalty

necessary

pillow
player
point (n.)
power (n.)
primitive
profession

reporter
respected

score (v.)
society
sophisticated

talent
term (n.)
tribe

valuable

Expressions

Good to see you.   No doubt about it.

CHAPTER SIX

alarm clock
amount (n.)
anymore
arrest (v.)

bowling
burglar

cabinet
cash (n.)

circus
crazy

director
disguise
doubt (v.)

examine

familiar

lasagna
liar

necessarily
note (v.)
notice (v.)

patch (n.)
promise (v.)

rare
real
reasonable
recognize
report (v.)

South American
stolen
surprise
suspect (v.)

theft
thief

wake up (v.)

Expressions

Give my regards to Tino.
I'll be glad to.

What's new?
How much is it worth?

I doubt it.
Not necessarily.

My car broke down.
I got stuck in a traffic jam.

CHAPTER SEVEN

absolutely
accurately
again
as

bet (v.)

car lot
champion
closed
comparison
competitively

dangerously
defeat (n.)
diet (n.)

easily
energetically
exercise (v.)

fight (n.)

grin (v.)

health

inside
interrupt

last (v.)
less
loser

mad
myself

neither

object (n.)
overweight

pet

regularly
rest (n.)

same (pron.)
scratch (v.)

seriously
sickness
sleep (n.)
sore (adj.)

trade (n.)
trade-in
trouble (n.)

weakness

Expressions

I'll bet he wins.
I'll do my best.

Get in shape.
How do you like my new hat?

What!

CHAPTER EIGHT

aside

brother-in-law
build

chance (n.)
character
cheer (v.)
chief (n.)
comfortably
custom

dress up

edge
electricity
embarrassed
event
excited
expansion

gather

hangout (n.)

importance
improve
island

middle
miserable
mother-in-law

native
news

offend
oppose
opposition

platform
present (adj.)
private (adj.)
progress (n.)

road

seem
someday
success
suggest

tax (n.)

wrestler

Expressions

Have you heard the news?
What are you talking about?

I know what you mean.
That's a good point.

It seems to me that . . .
It's a step backward.

That sounds good.
I'm looking forward to it.

There's one thing that bothers me.
He has terrible manners.

She's a pain in the neck.
She made my life miserable.

She's concerned about her looks.
I drive a beat-up car.

How can I break the ice?
What about me?

First of all . . .
After all . . .